*Clayoquot & Dissent*

British Columbia

Vancouver Island

Vancouver

Clayoquot
Sound

Victoria

# Clayoquot & Dissent

*Essays by*

TZEPORAH BERMAN

GORDON BRENT INGRAM

MAURICE GIBBONS

RONALD B. HATCH

LOŸS MAINGON

CHRISTOPHER HATCH

*Illustrations by*

MARGUERITE GIBBONS

RONSDALE/CACANADADADA

1994

RONSDALE PRESS LTD.
3350 West 21st Avenue
Vancouver, B.C.,Canada
V6S 1G7

Set in New Baskerville 11 pt on 14
Typesetting: The Typeworks, Vancouver, B.C.
Printing: Hignell Printing, Winnipeg, Manitoba
Cover Design: Cecilia Jang
Inside Photos: Sierra Legal Defence Fund
Map: Clayoquot Land Use Decision – 1993

The paper used in this book is Miami Vellum. It is recycled stock containing no dioxins. It is totally chlorine-free (TCF) as well as acid-free (therefore of archival quality). The paper is made from at least 10% post-consumer waste.

The publisher wishes to thank the Canada Council and the British Columbia Cultural Services Branch for their generous financial assistance.

CANADIAN CATALOGUING IN PUBLICATION DATA

Clayoquot and Dissent

ISBN 0-921870-29-9

1. Civil disobedience — British Columbia. 2. Clayoquot Sound Region (BC) — Environmental conditions. 3. Environmental policy — British Columbia — Clayoquot Sound Region. 4. Forest policy —British Columbia —Clayoquot Sound Region. I. Berman, Tzeporah, 1969-
FC3829.9.C62C62 1994      971.1'2      C94-910718-2
F1089.V3C62 1994

*To all those who
stood for the future of
Clayoquot Sound*

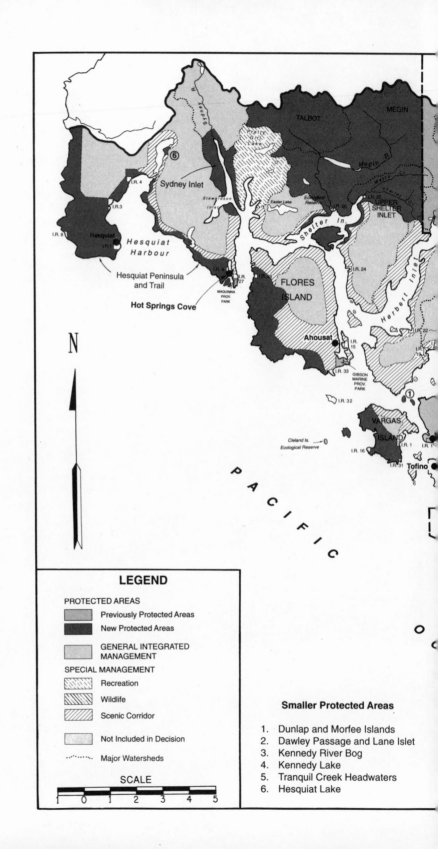

N

LEGEND

PROTECTED AREAS

Previously Protected Areas

New Protected Areas

GENERAL INTEGRATED MANAGEMENT

SPECIAL MANAGEMENT

Recreation

Wildlife

Scenic Corridor

Not Included in Decision

Major Watersheds

SCALE

1  0  1  2  3  4  5

Smaller Protected Areas

1. Dunlap and Morfee Islands
2. Dawley Passage and Lane Islet
3. Kennedy River Bog
4. Kennedy Lake
5. Tranquil Creek Headwaters
6. Hesquiat Lake

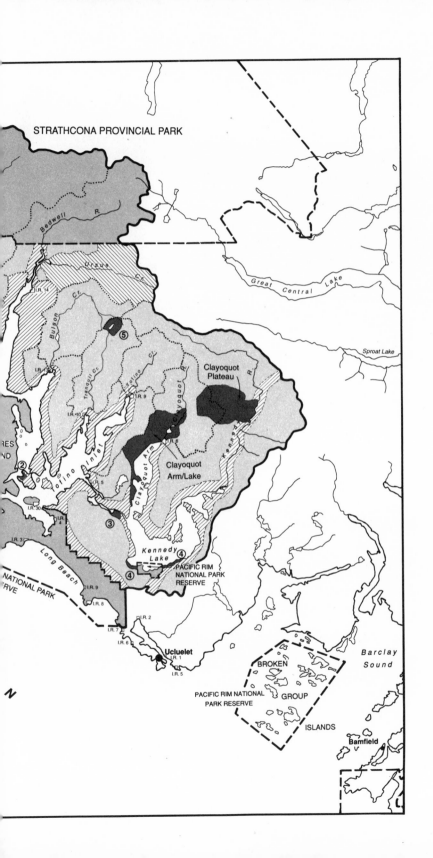

STRATHCONA PROVINCIAL PARK

Bedwell R.

Ursus Cr.

Great Central Lake

Sproat Lake

I.R. 14

Bulson Cr.

5

Clayoquot
Plateau

Tranquil Cr.

Tofino Cr.

Tofino R.

Clayoquot R.

Kennedy R.

I.R. 9

I.R. 40

I.R. 6

Clayoquot
Arm/Lake

RES
ND

2

Tofino Inlet

Clayoquot Arm

I.R. 5

I.R. 30

I.R.
4

3

I.R. 3

Long Beach

Kennedy
Lake

4

PACIFIC RIM
NATIONAL PARK
RESERVE

4

NATIONAL PARK
RVE

I.R. 9

I.R. 8

I.R. 2

I.R. 7

I.R. 6

Ucluelet

I.R. 1

I.R. 5

N

Barclay
Sound

BROKEN

PACIFIC RIM NATIONAL
PARK RESERVE

GROUP

ISLANDS

Bamfield

ACKNOWLEDGEMENTS

The contributors wish to thank Veronica Hatch for her editorial help in shaping the manuscript and for the long hours she spent researching the background to the Clayoquot protests. Our thanks go also to Erika Behrisch for her time and care in proofing the text.

We owe a debt of gratitude to the environmental organizations who opened their files and made accessible a mine of information, especially the Sierra Legal Defence Fund who gave permission to include the photographs of recent and ongoing logging violations in the Clayoquot.

We wish also to offer thanks to Tzeporah Berman for permission to use the back-cover photograph of Clayoquot Sound (the Hawaii of the north); to Aaron Klockars for his permission to use the front-cover photograph of the arrest; to Sue Gregory and Ian Parfitt of Western Canada Wilderness Committee for the use of their rich mapping resources; and to Valerie Langer of Friends of Clayoquot Sound, who supplied information about the early years of the protests.

Finally, we would like to offer our special thanks to Olga, who did so much for so many.

\* \* \*

Ronsdale Press is donating all profits from the sale of *Clayoquot & Dissent* to the protection of Clayoquot Sound.

CONTENTS

# Takin' it Back

Tzeporah Berman

*To brand as criminal many of our best and most conscientious idealists, can only increase the distance between people of conscience and the state. That would be very bad for our future.*
— Victoria Times-Colonist, Editorial, Oct. 20, 1993

The protests in Clayoquot Sound represent one of the largest civil disobedience actions in Canada's history. In the summer of 1993 over 800 people were arrested for standing on a logging road in one of the largest areas of temperate rainforest left in the world. Many were there for less than ten minutes. Hundreds have gone to jail. The people who protested in Clayoquot Sound have been referred to as "spoilt children," "welfare bums," "hippies" and most recently by Patrick Moore of the industry-funded "B.C. Forest Alliance" as "wacked out nature worshippers who pray to the moon." They have also been called heroes. In reality they were courageous grandmothers, children, students, seniors and others from all walks of life who found freedom in incarceration and strength in the ability to stand together and make change.

In 1969 the Canadian Council of Christians and Jews wrote that, "Law and order, though vital for society, can often be used to cover injustice. It is no longer sufficient merely to advocate obedience to law. The attainment of justice is first; without it, law is merely a facade."[1] Law is the product of an evolving process and as such it should reflect issues important to society. As values and perceptions change, the law must be recast to reflect new realities.[2] Throughout history, social conflict has proven necessary to attain dramatic social change. At one time blacks were treated as slaves and women were considered their husband's property. For many people who stood on the road in Clayoquot Sound, viewing "nature" as a commodity which humans have the right to exploit seems equally as absurd. Before thousands of black people were given their freedom or women were given the right to vote, there were the lunch counters and buses in the South and thousands of women jailed for picketing polling stations and chaining themselves to legislatures. Any attempt to reevaluate our basic perceptions of worth and value will not be easy and will not come without a dramatic struggle. For many, the catalyst necessary to begin to see the forests for the trees and to reevaluate our relationship with "nature" was the summer of 1993 in Clayoquot Sound.

Located on the west coast of Vancouver Island, Clayoquot (pronounced Klak'wat) Sound is one of very few areas of coastal lowland temperate rainforest left on the planet. It is a unique and beautiful region of white sand beaches, deep green valleys with rich salmon spawning streams, fjords, fresh water lakes, and snow-capped alpine mountains. Clayoquot Sound is home to ancient western red cedars over a thousand years old and Douglas firs that tower 250 feet above the ground. Because of its diverse geography, the area provides habitat for the black bear, cougar, wolves, bald eagles, the elusive marbled murrelet, orca and grey whales and some of the rarest sharks in the world.

Given its intense beauty and high "resource" value, it is not surprising that Clayoquot Sound has become the scene of a showdown of epic proportions. The protests in Clayoquot Sound began over a decade ago on Meares Island. After a two-year planning process, timber giant MacMillan Bloedel pulled out and refused all three options presented by the negotiators. When the logging boats headed out to the island, they were met with a blockade of Nuu-chah-nulth First Nations people and local environmentalists. Eventually the Nuu-chah-nulth obtained an injunction to prevent the company from logging the island, but the issue is still before the courts and has already cost the native community over a million dollars in legal fees.

The first protests were the beginning of a growing relationship between First Nations and the environmental community, a relationship that has matured considerably over the last year. Nonnative environmentalists are gradually coming to realize what had been obvious from the First Nations' perspective all along: people don't live in parks and an ancient burial ground is not a recreational site. While the environmental community has still much to learn, Clayoquot Sound has sparked a deeper understanding of the links between social and environmental issues. We are at a point of consensus between the environmental and native communities—that clearcutting irreparably damages our ecological, social and cultural landscapes.

The committees, government processes and subsequent blockades and protests continued intermittently over the years, but didn't reach a fever pitch until 1993, after the provincial government's announcement of the Clayoquot Land Use Decision. After much time and fanfare, Premier Harcourt announced that 62% of Clayoquot Sound would be open to clearcut logging; 33% of Clayoquot Sound would be "protected." What the Premier didn't say is that almost half of the protected area was previously protected and the 62% of Clayoquot Sound open to clearcut logging translates into 74% of the rainforest. Adding insult to injury, the government designated some areas of forests as "scenic corridors" and others as "special management zones." In reality, scenic corridors have proven to be thin strips of trees left along the water while the mountains above are stripped clean. For all intensive purposes "special management zones" appear to be another term for what was previously "modified landscape"—clearcuts.

Almost 70% of Vancouver Island's ancient forests have been

clearcut. Where there were once 170 intact watersheds on the island, now there are only eleven. Five are in Clayoquot Sound. Under the new decision, two intact watersheds would be protected. The decision was touted far and wide as a "responsible compromise." Before the decision, the industry was clearcutting 540,000 cubic metres of rainforest a year in Clayoquot Sound; after the decision they were allowed to log 600,000 cubic metres.

The Clayoquot Land Use Decision sparked cries of protest around the province which quickly spread around the globe. On July 1, the Clayoquot Sound Peace Camp opened and protests were held at Canadian consulates in Austria, Germany, England, Australia and the United States.

\* \* \*

*"As the moon set over the barren, stumpridden mountains each night, hope for the future grew with our numbers."*
— Amy Simpson, Peace Camp Organizer.

The Peace Camp was set up by the Friends of Clayoquot Sound to provide a meaningful forum for grassroots protests. It was a ramshackle village of tents and trailers symbolically situated in an old clearcut known as "the Black Hole." In the four months that it was operating, over 12,000 people visited the camp and joined the protests. In the Peace Camp we created a fluctuating, chaotic and warm community that functioned somewhat as a large extended family, through intense stress and upheaval. In this community, business people rolled up their sleeves beside students, musicians and doctors to wash dishes, help with twenty-four-hour security, or plan the protests to come. Functioning solely on donations, the camp managed to feed at least 200 people a day with healthy vegetarian meals.

In many respects the Peace Camp was a vehicle for and an embodiment of social change. Everyone who entered the camp agreed to abide by a basic set of principles that formed the foundations upon which the community functioned and the context within which we protested. The Peaceful Direct Action Code, as it was called, was developed through an analysis of the philosophies of nonviolent civil disobedience. It was built upon Gandhian principles and the lessons learned from civil rights and environmental protests around the globe. It is as follows:

Peaceful Direct Action Code

1. Our attitude is one of openness, friendliness and respect toward all beings we encounter.
2. We will not use violence either verbal or physical towards any being.
3. We will not damage any property and we will discourage others from doing so.
4. We will strive for an atmosphere of calm and dignity.
5. We will carry no weapons.
6. We will not bring or use alcohol or drugs.

Each day at the Camp, workshops were held which explored the philosophy of nonviolence and civil disobedience, consensus decision-making and legal issues, as well as the history and ecology of Clayoquot Sound. The workshops and "Peaceful Direct Action Code" helped to ensure that the massive protests and the camp community remained peaceful at all times. People learned how to work together, diffuse anger, to refocus fear and anxiety constructively, and most of all, to listen to and respect one another. The philosophy of nonviolence has a great deal to do with abolishing power as we know it and redefining it as something common to all. *Power over* is to be replaced by *shared power*, by the power to do things, by the discovery of our own strength as opposed to a passive receiving of power exercised by others, often in our name. Individuals feel, and in many ways are, powerless against the state, but when we are more than individuals we can find strength, confidence and real power in working together. The success of the Peace Camp was not only in the peaceful daily blockades at the Kennedy River Bridge but the skills, knowledge and experience that thousands of individuals took back to their communities. What grew out of the "Black Hole" was a common understanding that we have a right, indeed a responsibility, to stand up for what we believe in—and together we have the ability to do it effectively.

The government and industry have responded to the protests with fear and aggression. They have called environmentalists "hysterical," and worse. We've heard this before. They took a similar line up to the day the Atlantic cod stocks collapsed. For years Dupont called environmentalists "hysterical" for claiming that CFC's eat away at the ozone layer. Our challenge is to reverse the burden of proof. It is the corporations and governments who now must prove that their practices are ecologically and culturally responsible.

Government and industry have characterized the present debate as a choice between liking trees or liking workers. But the thousands of people who came to Clayoquot realized that we simply cannot negate our dependence on natural systems; scientists call it biodiversity. "Biodiversity is no frill. It is life and all that sustains life."[3] Biodiversity resembles a hammock: as destructive industrial practices like clearcutting dramatically alter existing ecosystems, species go extinct, the hammock unravels. Eventually the hammock can no longer hold anything. We need to begin to understand our dependence on natural systems and to develop mechanisms to have this understanding translate into socio-economic and political realities.

Ultimately, the struggle for Clayoquot Sound is not only a struggle for "wilderness" or sound forest practices but fundamentally a struggle with how we interact with the natural world; and whether we have a right to irreversibly change, and in some cases irreversibly damage the environment. It is a struggle to value the future over monetary gain and, in so doing, to recognize that short-term economic gain will not benefit human or non-human communities. It is a struggle for justice. And may be no more complicated than simply recognizing that we all need to breathe air and drink water.

The essays that follow combine experiential knowledge with academic and scientific understandings to provide a critical analysis of the struggle for Clayoquot Sound and the legal system in which hundreds have been entangled as a result of their dissent. This is a powerful book that rings with the voices of many and exists as a testament to the power of community and our passion for survival. The message rings clear: When we stand, we stand for our lives.

*Tzeporah*

August, 1994

### Notes

1. Canadian Council of Christians and Jews. *A Report of the International Conference of Christians and Jews*, 1969, p. 21.

2. For a more thorough discussion of law and environmental ethics, see Christopher Stone, "Should Trees Have Standing?—Toward Legal Rights For Natural Objects," *Southern California Law Review*, 45:450, p. 461; and Christopher Tribe, "Ways Not to Think About Plastic Trees: New Foundations for Environmental Law," *The Yale Law Journal*, 83:7 (1974), p. 1342.

3. Douglas Chadwick, 1991. "Conserving Biodiversity: A Unified Approach," in *Landscape Linkages and Biodiversity*, Island Press, Washington, D.C.

# The Ecology of a Conflict

GORDON BRENT INGRAM, PH.D.[1]

## I.   Chronicle of a Conflict

1979, September
Concerned citizens of Clayoquot Sound form "Friends of Clayoquot Sound" in response to rumours that Meares Island is to be logged.

1980
Clearcut logging expands rapidly from the southeast of the Clayoquot Sound area along Kennedy Lake.[2]

1984
Blockade by Clayoquot Sound residents, the Nuu-chah-nulth and supporters on Meares Island. Meares Island Tribal Park declared.

1985, March
The Tla-o-qui-aht and Ahousaht obtain an injunction which stops logging on Meares Island.

1988, June to September
Blockades of Sulphur Pass by concerned residents of Tofino. 35 people arrested.

**1989, January**
Members of Friends of Clayoquot Sound and other residents clean up Nestucca oil spill. Many of these residents, who are praised for their heroic efforts by the Province, are later imprisoned for their activities in the Sulphur Pass blockades.

**1989**
Sentencing of Sulphur Pass blockaders, who are imprisoned for up to 45 days.

**1990, Spring**
The first agreement in principle for conservation partnership takes place between the Nuu-chah-nulth and Ecotrust.

**1991, January 31**
The initial recommendations of the Clayoquot Sound Sustainable Development Task Force are introduced.[3]

**1991, May**
A number of participants in the advisory groups associated with the Task Force withdraw because of perceived biases against conservation in its organizational structure.[4]

**1991, July**
A report on "life support services and natural diversity" of the Strategy for Sustainable Development for Clayoquot Sound[5] is tabled.

**1991, September**
Bulson River Road blockade. Six arrested on SLAPP suit (Strategic Lawsuit against Public Participation).

**1991, October**
The New Democratic Party forms the new provincial government. Michael Harcourt becomes premier.

**1991, late**
The First Draft of the Clayoquot Sound Sustainable Development Strategy[6] is circulated.

**1992, Summer**
A blockade for over 5 months at Clayoquot Arm Bridge, with

65 people arrested.[7]

1992, December

A report to Premier Harcourt is made by J. H. Walker (an Assistant Deputy Minister of Environment and Chairman of the Clayoquot Sound Strategy Committee) and Robert Prescott-Allen (Committee Director) recommending "some logging in the sensitive rain forests...while further study is conducted."[8]

1993, January 14

A failure of consensus by the Steering Committee process for the Clayoquot Sustainable Development Task Force[9] occurs. The Minister of Forests and the Office of the Premier refer the reports of the Steering Committee to other agencies within the provincial government, including the Port Alberni office of the Ministry of Forests. A plan (what will be the April 1993 decision), that grants high rates of cutting for the coming five years in order to maintain investor confidence in MacMillan Bloedel Ltd., is thrown together in the subsequent eight weeks.

1993, January

A globally-oriented network for conservation of the Clayoquot[10] is formed.

1993, February

The Government of British Columbia buys shares in MacMillan Bloedel Ltd. and for a time holds one of the largest stakes. An inquiry is held, which concludes that there was no wrong doing.

1993, March

FOCS campaign in Europe. Major European groups begin showing interest in Clayoquot Sound.

1993, April 13

The Government of British Columbia announces the April 1993 decision—"The Clayoquot Sound Land Use Decision"—which claims to balance the environmental, economic and social needs of the area. The decision is supposed to be without prejudice to aboriginal treaty negotiations on Vancouver Island.[11]

1993, April 22

The Commission on Resources and Environment (CORE) releases the *Public Report and Recommendations Re: Issues Arising from the Government's Clayoquot Sound Land Use Decision.*[12]

1993, April

A new forest industries public-relations programme, directed at Europe, is initiated and represents a new level of globalization in the conflict over the Clayoquot.

1993, June 1

The report, *Government of British Columbia Response to the Commission on Resources and Environment's Public Report and Recommendations Regarding Issues Arising from the Clayoquot Land Use Decision,*[13] is released.

1993, June 2

The recommendations for new "Clayoquot Sound Forest Practices"[14] are released.

1993, July 1

The Peace Camp opens in the "Black Hole" off the Kennedy Lake Road. Demonstrations in sympathy in consumer countries: Austria, Germany, United Kingdom, and U.S.A.

1993, July 5

First day at blockades in Clayoquot Sound. No arrests are made, but Federal M.P. Svend Robinson, Belgian M.E.P. Paul Staes, and others block road. One year later, Robinson is charged and sentenced to 14 days in jail.

1993, July 6

Three grandmothers arrested on the blockade and jailed for refusing to sign the terms of the release. They spend over three months in jail.

1993, July 15
   Australian rock band, Midnight Oil, flies into Clayoquot
   Sound, meets the Nuu-chah-nulth leaders and performs at
   the Peace Camp. 5,000 people join the blockades. MacMillan
   Bloedel does not attempt to cross the bridge.

1993, July 16
   Protest organizer Tzeporah Berman falsely arrested from the
   side of the road, and charged with "aiding and abetting."

1993, July
   Western Canada Wilderness Committee (WCWC) begins
   building its "Witness Trail" into Clayoquot Sound, with permission from the Ha-o-qui-aht First Nations.

1993, July 19
   The media campaign intensifies in the United States and
   Europe in support of greater conservation of the ancient for-
   est in Clayoquot,[15] and there is intervention by Robert
   Kennedy Jr. of the Washington-based Natural Resources
   Defense Council.

1993, July 19
   Release of CORE's recommendations, *Public Participation in
   Implementation* of *Government Clayoquot Sound Land Use
   Decision.*[16]

1993, August 9
   A mass arrest at the blockade of over 300 people.[17]

1993, September
   Additional arrests of demonstrators in September and
   October. Multiple demonstrations at the B.C. Legislative
   Buildings, protesting both logging of ancient forests and ar-
   rests of protestors.

1993, September
   First caravan arrives in Clayoquot from St. John's,
   Newfoundland.

1993, September
WCWC extracts a huge cedar stump, "Stumpy," from a clearcut in Clayoquot Sound and sends it on a tour across Canada and Europe.

1993, October 4
Peace Camp closes. National and International campaign intensifies.

1993, October 13
Renewed demonstrations in front of the B.C. legislature in support of the people on trial for defying the court injunction against the blockade.[18]

1993, October 14
The first of the "tough" jail sentences is issued for the 44 protesters who violated the court order against the blockades.[19] Demonstrations the following day outside the Vancouver Courthouse.

1993, October 20
Fifteen demonstrators charged with trespassing, after occupying the federal Conservative Party's downtown headquarters[20] in Ottawa.

1993, October 25
The "B.C. government would welcome Liberal intervention in Clayoquot."[21] (The Liberal Party of Canada won the Federal election, with such prominent figures as Paul Martin having talked of federal intervention to end the conflict and to make the area a National Park.)

1993, October 28
"Now Chretien backing off Clayoquot."[22]

1993, October 31
"About 200 protesters urged prime minister designate Jean Chrétien to keep his promise to end logging in B.C.'s Clayoquot Sound...."[23]

1993, October
> The Province of B.C. announces its willingness, for the first time, to recognize and negotiate with the representatives of the Nuu-chah-nulth Nations.

1993, October
> One of the responses of the British Columbia Commission on Resources and the Environment (CORE) to the April 1993 decision is a recommendation for a scientific panel,[24] which is established months later.[25]

1993, October
> The Premier, Michael Harcourt, announces a $2 million grant to the University of British Columbia Faculty of Forestry, in large part because of its support for his positions on logging in B.C.

1993, November 9
> Greenpeace International blockade at Kennedy River Bridge. Arrests also at Canadian consulates in Germany and Austria.

1993, November 10
> Second Clayoquot Caravan arrives from St. John's. FOCS goes to Japan to persuade companies not to buy forest products from Clayoquot.

1993, November
> The 1993 Blockade near Kennedy Lake ends.

1993, November 12
> A Provincial Ombudsman report says the Province "failed to consult the Nuu-chah-nulth First Nations in a meaningful and timely manner"[26] in the April 1993 Cabinet decision.

1993, November
> A Forest Practices Code[27] is proposed for British Columbia.

1993, December
> Increased concern in Europe for the logging and land-use practices in Clayoquot Sound.[28]

**1993, December 10**

A tentative agreement is reached for an "Interim Measures Agreement between British Columbia and the Hereditary Chiefs of the Central Region, Nuu-chah-nulth Tribes," with ratification planned for March 1994.[29]

**1994, February**

Michael Harcourt, Premier of British Columbia, travels to Europe,[30] along with representatives of the Nuu-chah-nulth Nation,[31] and denies that clearcut logging in Clayoquot Sound is environmentally destructive. He claims that all of the needed changes to logging practices in the area have already occurred. Greenpeace protests in Europe against "Mr. Clearcut."

**1994, February 9**

Release of the Commission on Resources and Environment (CORE) recommendations for Vancouver Island with a proposed cut in timber output throughout the area.[32] These recommendations do not extend to Clayoquot Sound.

**1994, March**

The first cancellation of pulp contracts in the U.K. (by Scott Paper and Kimberly-Clark) with companies operating in Clayoquot Sound.[33]

**1994, March 19**

Signing of the "Interim Measures Agreement between Her Majesty the Queen In Right of the Province of British Columbia and The Hawiih of the Tla-o-qui-aht First Nations, the Ahousaht First Nation, the Hesquiaht First Nation, the Toquaht First Nation and the Ucluelet First Nation."[34]

**1994, March**

Discussion begins in the B.C. legislature on the first B.C. Forest Practices Code.

**1994, July**

Clearcut logging continues in Clayoquot Sound at rapid rates with little change. The Government of British

Columbia admits that it will be at least two years before new standards and practices, as alternatives to clearcutting, are implemented. The Minister of Forests also backtracks on his commitment to decrease the annual allowable cut in B.C.[35] (which he had earlier admitted was unsustainably high)— confirming that little has actually improved, so far, in terms of protection of old-growth forest ecosystems.

1994, July

Greenpeace releases a paper confirming "the worst." As of July 1994, much of the cutting going on in Clayoquot Sound still involves clearcut logging operations that are illegal and that supposedly had been stopped.[36]

1994, August

MV Greenpeace sails into Clayoquot, hosts "historic meeting" of Nuu-chah-nulth, Greenpeace and MacMillan Bloedel representatives for a discussion of alternative harvesting methods.

1994, September

By late summer, the continuing problems in Clayoquot Sound are temporarily out of the public's mind.[37] Clearcut logging continues at a rapid pace.

## II.   Intersecting Crises

Conflict in Clayoquot Sound, as the above chronology indicates, has been developing for over a decade. The issues, the organizations, the bureaucracies, the corporations, the communities, and the different perspectives of the people involved are numerous. In rough and ready terms, the conflict is between corporate clearcut logging and conservation of some of the largest remaining areas of temperate rainforest. Yet reducing the conflict so simplistically does not allow for an understanding that could lead to a resolution of this ongoing conflict. Such a logger versus conservation dichotomy not only omits any investigation of the unique and complex features of the Sound, it also prevents us from looking at the ways in which decisions were made for the Sound's use, decisions which arose from personal ambitions, ineptness, dysfunctional bureaucracies, and corruption. As soon as one looks closely at the situation, a multitude of questions arise.

What problems compelled thousands of people to disrupt logging operations in British Columbia throughout 1993 at the risk of facing criminal charges in the Supreme Courts of British Columbia? What pressures caused the B.C. Ministry of Forests and its affiliates to rush through a land-use plan in early 1993 with very little information, almost no commitment to improved environmental management, and indifference to the fact that their plan accelerated rates of liquidation in our old-growth forests? What political intrigues forced the Cabinet of the Government of B.C., in April 1993, to accept a compromise land-use plan even when it involved destruction of a globally recognized resource? What caused MacMillan Bloedel Ltd., the largest company in the area and major beneficiary of the land-use decision, to press for charges of criminal, rather than civil, contempt against the Clayoquot activists? How did the provincial government develop a land management bureaucracy with a colonial bias capable of such a misuse of science? What kept the Nuu-chah-nulth First Nations and environmental groups from cooperating until it was almost too late? How has this brief conflict so permanently altered political alliances in B.C.?

One way of answering these questions is to study the conflict of Clayoquot Sound as an ecology. The concept of ecology is normally applied to nature, but it can also help to illuminate the web of interests in the Clayoquot. Ecology is about relationships. It is from the ancient Greek word *oikos* for "house" or "household." This investigation, then, is about a "house" in conflict on the central west coast of Vancouver Island. It is about the sum total of natural and social relationships and the contradictions and conflicts that have emerged in recent years around timber harvesting, nearly all of which involve a set of logging practices called "clearcutting."[38] Most importantly, aside from the Nuu-chah-nulth retaking control of their lands, this story is about a new chapter in the struggle for the authentic and viable conservation of natural habitats with relatively intact temperate rainforest, shore, and shallow marine ecosystems.

It would be an understatement to say that the conflict in the "house" of Clayoquot Sound is over ideas, "systems of knowledge,"[39] and "paradigm[40] shifts."[41] It is remarkable that there has been so little bloodshed in a situation where thousands of hectares of primary temperate rainforest are being rapidly liquidated. Over 800 demonstrators, practising nonviolent civil disobedience,[42] have been found guilty of criminal contempt by the Courts of British Columbia. Many have gone to jail. The conflict does not yet have an ending, but it has taken a sudden turn with the tentative agreement of the First Nations communities of Clayoquot, the Nuu-chah-nulth, with the Province of British Columbia.

The ecology I am investigating is one of neo-colonialism in the guise of corporate logging that purports to be "development." It also concerns "environmentalism" controlled by non-native groups that sometimes forget issues of cultural difference, local control, and hereditary title. The history of the ecology of conflict in Clayoquot Sound goes back at least two centuries, and concerns the discounting and devaluing of First Nations' perspectives and their unsuccessful efforts at preserving their culture with its ecological relationships. It is also about current difficulties in bridging gaps between traditional/local and more global science-based perspectives, as well as the intensifying struggle of the Nuu-chah-nulth communities to define conservation areas in terms of their own needs and perspectives.[43] The ecology of a conflict also involves globalizing capital, logging companies, such as B.C.-grown MacMillan Bloedel Ltd. and International Forest Products, the myriad forms of support and subsidies provided by the government, the increasing pressures for large profits, and the difficulties of shifting to sustainable and diversified production. Finally, the ecology includes the complacency, inertia, and indifference of the various governments and current political groupings in British Columbia and Canada which continues to this day.

In the following analysis, I shall be drawing on my own research[44] in the Clayoquot in the years leading up to the April 1993 decision. The discussion will proceed in the following order. First, I will examine how Clayoquot became a landscape of conflict. This in turn will lead to a consideration of the global significance of these island ecosystems with their ancient forests, as well as the implications of liquidating these complex mosaics of old-growth forest ecosystems. I will then look at the stakeholders, the various groups with an interest in the area. This leads to a discussion of the background and main proposals of the April 1993 decision of the Cabinet of B.C. The environmental standards in the Cabinet proposal are then compared to international standards for conservation planning, to show how the Clayoquot decision ran counter to all currently acceptable approaches to conservation and sustainable development. The anti-conservation biases of the various provincial bureaucracies are then considered. This leads me to offer a list of issues that must be better resolved if we are to avert future confrontations. Finally, some approaches to supporting the conservation efforts of the Nuu-chah-nulth, the rightful owners of Clayoquot Sound, are suggested.

## III.  *Downward Spirals and Ecosystems of Conflict*

When one begins to itemize the components of an ecology dominated by conflict, it is important to step back so as to recognize some of the larger forces that are simply too big to be seen up-close. First, there is no doubt that the trajectory of the sum total of human and natural relationships lies in the direction of impoverishment and "underdevelopment." The second point is that competition for dwindling natural resources—timber, in this case—takes up an increasing proportion of the energy and resources of local social and ecological systems. To borrow from ecosystem dynamics, one can say that the system is becoming entropic, with energy dissipated instead of concentrated, as social and biotic components atrophy and are lost.

In ecosystems where conflict prevails, the internal dynamics be-come simplified and didactic, so as to create a "downward spiral" typical of frontiers such as the increasingly impoverished mountain villages of Nepal or the resource frontiers of Amazonia.[45] With Clayoquot Sound, the same dynamic operates, but since Clayoquot Sound lies in a "developed" country, we find more rapid and "efficient" destruction of complex natural ecosystems. This destruction also occurs with fewer people using more ex-pensive technology—and with greater concentrations of profit. In the struggle to protect the world's remaining primary rain-forests, the conflict over Clayoquot has been exceptional in two ways. There has been very little violence. But in comparison to the conflicts over tropical rainforests in very poor countries, the contentions around the use and abuse of scientific information, as the basis for what should have been rational land-use planning, have been heightened.

The alternative to an ecosystem dominated by conflict is one characterized by cooperation. Ecosystems of cooperation have checks and balances so that competition (and resource losses and disruptions associated with it) does not destabilize the entire sys-tem. Ecosystems based on cooperation also have more formalized rights to resources and corresponding management responsibili-ties involving a wider set of communities and social groups. The unresolved Native land claims of the Clayoquot, which began to be considered only in October 1993, are too problematic for the stable management of resources. As more and more of the wealth and renewable resources are wasted on conflict, there is an im-poverishment which exacerbates the conflicts, a feature which has been highly visible in the Clayoquot over the last few years. Once there is a downward spiral, it takes increasingly more social resources, often including subsidies from other areas, before there is hope for renewed productivity, biological richness, and efficiency.

Although the British Columbia Cabinet's so-called "compro-mise" for Clayoquot Sound (the April 1993 decision) was in-tended to give the impression of reconciling conflict, in fact the

decision intensified it. The April 1993 decision[46] did not establish a sustainable programme of timber harvesting and conservation. Equally important, the compromise failed to take into
account the rights of the indigenous peoples of the area. In effect, the compromise can be seen as one aspect of the crisis of
"decolonization." In the period before the "compromise," the
Nuu-chah-nulth communities had been struggling without success to assert their own conservation and development priorities
in the face of some of the most rapid removal of ancient forest
ever seen in temperate zones. But they were unable to be heard.
Without their presence in the discussions, environmental groups
such as Western Canada Wilderness Committee and Friends of
Clayoquot Sound entered the arena to fill a political vacuum. But
the contradiction remained that these largely urban, non-native
groups could not speak for the rightful owners of the area.

The "compromise decision" also occurred at a time when the
community at large was beginning to change its sense of how we
ought to recognize, represent and value our ecological relations
and natural resources. As our old-growth forests are removed, we
are faced with critical decisions about the balance we will maintain between irreplacable ecosystems and exploitation of those
systems as natural resources. The concept of biodiversity,[47] important as it is, only hints at complex natural phenomena and the
social needs for their utilization and conservation. The technical
side of the problem also involves a crisis in site planning and the
need to consider decisions with multiple scales, from the site to
the broader landscape.

In effect, the April 1993 Clayoquot decision demonstrates the
inability of both provincial and federal governments to make the
fundamental changes necessary to grant First Nations control
over the land they inhabit and the resources on it. Even the 1994
Interim Measures Agreement between the Nuu-chah-nulth and
the B.C. government, which was intended to grant native peoples
a voice in the destiny of their lands, has functioned as a way to
buy more time while the area continues to be logged. It is this
continuing logging, the pushing of roads into pristine water-

sheds, without a full examination of the consequences, that caused people from all over the world to take to the barricades. To understand what roused people to collective action in the largest act of civil disobedience in Canadian history, we need to examine the special characteristics of Clayoquot Sound.

## IV. Islands on Islands: an Ecological Overview of Clayoquot Sound

Clayoquot Sound is incredibly beautiful, and for that reason alone, many would claim that it needs to be protected. The scientist does not ignore the beauty of the area, but goes one step beyond to recognize that the beauty derives from its unique features, features that give the Clayoquot tremendous global significance. There are few areas left in the North Pacific with such diverse mosaics of ecosystems of the shallow marine, shore, and ancient forest types. Many similar areas on the British Columbia coast have already been radically altered by clearcut timber harvesting. Clayoquot is sufficiently unusual and rich in the global context to deserve full environmental reviews of industrial operations, with an emphasis on preservation for as much of this intact system as possible. Yet the rush to complete and announce the April 1993 decision led to an inadequate review and an insubstantial report.

Since the government did not review the area properly, a brief overview of some of the Sound's more important features is necessary. Although many people, when they think of Clayoquot Sound, think first of the large watersheds with their huge trees, one has only to consult a map to see that much of the Sound comprises an archipelago of islands. Indeed, the area itself is part of an island—Vancouver Island. Islands with large tracts of primary rainforest constitute a distinct complex of terrestrial and marine ecosystems, with global significance, because of high levels of biological richness or, in the case of oceanic islands, the evolutionary distinctiveness of the organisms that they support.

Clayoquot Sound supports relatively new ecosystems[48] formed since the last glaciation, but also has some of the most extensive and complex rainforest and shallow marine ecosystems in the temperate latitudes. The myriad of small habitat units makes these settings prone to "fragmentation,"[49] and thus problematic for the conservation of biological diversity. Most of the remaining examples of islands with primary rainforest are in the Pacific Rim, particularly in Indonesia, Canada, Papua New Guinea, and Chile. All are threatened by intensive timber harvesting, mining and tourism. Considerably more inventorying, protection and monitoring of the remaining islands are needed.[50]

The forests of Clayoquot Sound, especially those near the coast, are what is called "temperate rainforests." There are modest parallels between humid tropical forests and the temperate rainforests of the North Pacific coast:

1. high levels of standing biomass;
2. complexity of forest structures, gaps and edges;
3. relatively heterogeneous mosaics of small habitat units which are fragmentation-prone; and
4. the importance of shore areas to terrestrial and shallow marine food webs.

In both cases, there is a subset of forest species associated with successional mosaics dominated by large, old trees, either standing or fallen, along with complex structures such as nesting cavities. Even though these species often utilize "old-growth"[51] ecosystems and habitat attributes, the evidence about how necessary such habitats are for their survival is inconclusive.

Marine areas adjacent to islands, as in the Clayoquot, often rival terrestrial zones in biological diversity. The structure of these marine ecosystems has not been comprehensively categorized.[52] The ecological boundaries of islands are not limited to shores and shallow marine areas. A shoreline is a zone of overlap between terrestrial and marine food webs, involving a distinct and added set of habitats. The shape of these habitat units are usually long and narrow, and therefore prone to breakup in times of environmental change.

Island ecosystems, such as those that make up Clayoquot, are especially vulnerable to industrial damage because of their many "soft" boundaries and gradients. In order to ensure that these ecosystems remain intact and functioning, careful monitoring and a high level of regulation of industrial practices and tourism is necessary. Moreover, the small size of most groupings of island habitats and the permeable nature of most of the boundaries can provide us with clues on how to maintain and rebuild many other natural ecosystems as expanding land use turns all remaining natural habitats in the world into "islands in a storm" of degrading regional environment. The remaining islands with primary rainforests require an international response, not only for their uniqueness, but also for what they can teach us about ecosystems under stress.

## V. The Age of Clearcutting: Dwindling Wilderness and Biological Diversity on the Pacific Rim

Although further studies on the islands of the Clayoquot are required, these studies are being sidelined because of the tremendous economic incentive to log coastal lowland rainforest. Given human population densities in coastal areas, lowland forests near the sea and along waterways have largely been cleared or altered. Remaining forests close to water access have become particularly attractive for commercial timber harvesting. Nearly all primary forests on accessible islands outside nature reserves will be liquidated through logging concessions or agricultural clearing in the coming decade. This is already the case in much of the Philippines.[53] British Columbia has not been immune to the environmental problems associated with underdevelopment, particularly in the marginal regions that possess few economic options. The capital necessary to establish logging activities in remote areas usually requires intensive extractive operations. Over the last two decades, the pressure for high rates of profit has been the major obstacle to development of effective frameworks for conservation of primary forest habitat and the establishment of authentic integrated management, which would support aboriginal land use and wilderness recreation.

The history of human impact on organisms, particularly species which are terrestrial, is one of ecological disaster and "extreme increases in instability and entropy."[54] More than 80% of the vertebrates which have gone extinct since 1600 A.D. have been endemic to oceanic islands. The responses of shore zones to land use vary with practices and biophysical settings, as well as the patterns of sediment transport. There are a number of key pathways for the cumulative transmission of disturbances from terrestrial areas to adjacent marine zones, and few for the transfer of on-site perturbations in marine areas onto the land. Terrestrially derived disturbances, such as clearcut logging operations, often involve the soil mantle, alterations of fresh-water regimens, and the deposition of suspended sediment in the sea. On the steep slopes of British Columbia, for example, clearcut logging operations cause large amounts of soil to be carried into the ocean beds, often altering the marine patterns substantially.

Most of the world's islands that were dominated by mosaics of primary rainforest were radically altered in the nineteenth and twentieth centuries. There was no lowland forest on oceanic islands not totally altered or converted within a century of European intrusion. Four sets of human impacts pose the largest threats to the biological diversity of the remaining islands with primary rainforest:

1. conversion and alteration of primary rainforest;
2. fragmentation of natural habitats, particularly in forested areas;
3. the impacts of terrestrial land use on marine areas; and
4. generalized degradation of the marine environment.

All four categories of impact can produce rapid but long-lasting synergistic and relatively island-wide changes. Both islands and moist forest on islands are under-represented in internationally recognized protected areas, even though they could provide relatively secure sites for long-term monitoring and control of disturbance. Unfortunately, all possibilities of protection have been jeopardized in recent years by global warming and possible sea-level rise.

A long-term threat to the continuing evolution of, and prospect for, successful management of island biotas is the disruption of patterns of colonization across entire archipelagoes. As natural habitats and respective populations on mainlands and adjacent islands decline, the distance/time ratios for recolonization increase. Connectivity and colonization pathways should therefore be major criteria in planning protected areas within archipelagoes.

Insularization has been compounded by inevitable fluctuations and unpredictable events with even greater losses of vulnerable habitat. Human beings are making virtually all islands more like isolated "oceanic" islands, which are relatively depauperate and which derive much of their global significance, in terms of biodiversity, from the endemic organisms that have persisted and evolved over long periods of relative stability and isolation. With the clearcut logging of Clayoquot Sound, stability in the ecosystem is virtually impossible to maintain, particularly in tiny, fragmented protected areas.

Relatively pristine islands with complex forest mosaics, such as Meares and Flores islands in the Clayoquot, may well become the central metaphor for "Nature" and conservation in coming decades. Yet archipelagoes within archipelagoes saturated with biological richness and linked by highly permeable membranes—as is the case with marine areas—are perpetually vulnerable to both isolation and disturbances generated from adjacent industrial activities. Even if pressures for logging and mining are removed by establishing national parks, programmes of inventorying and monitoring must be quickly initiated.[55]

While the impacts of logging and tourism suggest that large, multiple-use management units with small, pristine cores are inevitable in many areas, Clayoquot Sound could have been a strategic exception. With enough site-specific inventory data, the province could have provided impact assessment, mitigation formulations, and incremental conservation planning. The only thing needed was the political will to make conservation, both ecological and cultural, the over-riding priority for "eco-development."[56]

Given what has happened to date—with continued clearcutting and only weak improvements for environmental protection—it would seem that biosphere reserve status[57] might offer the Government of British Columbia the face-saving transition to an effective network of conservation and monitoring of biological diversity.[58] But the insufficient and badly designed core protected areas in the April 1993 decision and the rapid and broad fragmentation from the current logging practices will persist and stymie prospects of secure conservation of biodiversity, representative ecosystems, and natural processes across landscapes. Such an international designation, administered through the Man and the Biosphere Programme, could allow for a range of preservation and conservation options through highly protected cores and carefully managed buffers and corridors. This is sufficiently flexible to allow for adaptive management of the terrestrial-marine interface within which the cores and habitat "islands" are protected. The greatest advantage of the biosphere reserves system is the potential for sharing information in terms of particular ecosystems and environmental settings, such as islands with rainforest. The global monitoring potential of biosphere reserves has become a major component of the programme. Certainly such reserves in Clayoquot Sound would ensure that the highest standards are applied to the area, and such standards are essential if the current rulings in the 1993 decision are to be countered. But biosphere reserve status for Clayoquot Sound without a new land use plan, with gazetted demarcations based on principles of conservation biology and landscape ecology, would make a mockery of the entire international system at a time when there are growing pressures to ensure that such areas provide models for authentic balances between conservation and local development.

## *VI.  Stakeholders and the Engines of Conflict*

In analyzing the forces that created the 1993 conflict around Clayoquot, I am creating a 3-dimensional matrix, comprising people (grouped as "stakeholders"), land/resources, and time. The earlier chronicle tells us about time, whereas the previous outline of island ecosystems is about land and resources. But what about people? The conflict around Clayoquot, first and foremost, is about differences among groups of people.

The following is a list of the major stakeholders for Clayoquot Sound. By more fully appreciating the particular nature of their interests, priorities, and historical involvements, there may be more of a basis for negotiating authentic "compromise."

THE HAWIIH OF THE FIRST NATIONS OF CLAYOQUOT SOUND

- the Nuu-chah-nulth Nations' office in Port Alberni
- the Tla-o-qui-aht First Nations
- the Ahousaht First Nation
- the Hesquiaht First Nation
- the Toquaht First Nation
- the Ucluelet First Nation

There are several Nuu-chah-nulth communities, all with participation and representation in the Port Alberni office, and linked through family ties. Between and within these communities is a wide range of involvements in traditional land and marine tenure and cultural activities, and serious disparities in incomes, employment prospects, and access to social services.

OTHER LOCAL GROUPS

• Aside from the Nuu-chah-nulth communities, most other local residents have come relatively recently and many have not been in the area for more than a decade or two. While there are many local organizations, one of the few with much history and involvement in the area is the Friends of Clayoquot Sound. It was founded in 1979 by residents of the Sound who became concerned about the logging in their "back yard." They became especially active when rumours began to circulate that Meares Island was slated to be logged. They have pointed out that of the 250 direct logging jobs in Clayoquot Sound, only seven are held by residents of the Sound. The FOCS have actively fought to preserve the Sound. They organized the Peace Camp and blockades in the Summer of 1993.

ECONOMIC GROUPS

• MacMillan Bloedel Ltd. is the largest timber harvesting corporation in British Columbia and was established here in the early part of this century. The large majority of the rights to harvest timber in Clayoquot Sound are held by "MB." International Forest Products Ltd. has the only other major block of cutting rights in Clayoquot.

• The largest union in Clayoquot is the International Woodworkers of America. This union has been remarkably weak in countering job losses from automation and has tended to scapegoat the few modest new parks, as well as "environmentalists," as the reason for the decline in jobs. A small portion of these union locals have Nuu-chah-nulth members.

• A movement that receives much of its financial backing from the large corporations is composed of the Share groups,[59] which purport to want a kind of "balanced" use of land and resources. In fact, they emphasize short-term industrial extraction, at the expense of First Nations groups, who are attempting to maintain traditional ownership and land stewardship, and conservationists and "preservationists" committed to viable protection of a range of resources leading to "sustainable development."

• There is also a range of fishing and aquaculture interests, some of which have objectives compatible with better conservation.

• There are sportfishing and (eco)tourism outfitters who depend on high quality natural environments for their livelihoods. Some of these individuals are Nuu-chah-nulth and others are newcomers.

LOCAL GOVERNMENT GROUPS

• The District of Tofino is at the southern end of Clayoquot Sound.

• The Village of Ucluelet is adjacent to the most southerly edge of the Sound, actually on the ocean, and almost totally dependent on logging in Clayoquot for the livelihoods of local residents.

• The City of Port Alberni is a long distance from Clayoquot Sound, but because adjacent areas have been depleted of old-growth timber it is increasingly dependent on wood from Clayoquot for jobs in the mills.

• The Alberni-Clayoquot Regional District was also involved in many of the discussions on land use in Clayoquot Sound.

GOVERNMENT AGENCIES[60]

• Until recent years, the B.C. Ministry of Forests has tended to dominate the land-use planning and monitoring in Clayoquot Sound.

• Most of the decisions on land use in Clayoquot Sound by the B.C. Ministry of Environment have been subverted by associated ministries interested in short-term resource extraction. Consequently, the design processes for establishment of protected areas by the Ministry's agency, Parks B.C., have tended to be dominated more by pressures for short-term economic activities than by conservation biology or sound principles of environmental planning.

• The B.C. Ministry of Tourism has had varying levels of involvement in land-use planning and has been active in the decisions for Clayoquot in terms of mitigation of the negative impacts of clearcut logging. So far, this "visual resources management" has only been mildly successful.

• The B.C. Ministry of Regional and Economic Development coordinated the unsuccessful efforts for a strategy for sustainable development for Clayoquot.

• The B.C. Ministry of Aquaculture and Fisheries tended to promote the establishment of fish farms in sheltered inlets. This has often been in conflict with interests for both conservation and tourism.

• Parks Canada and Environment Canada became established in the management of the Pacific Rim National Park over twenty years ago and have considered adding parts of Clayoquot Sound to the park.

• Fisheries and Oceans Canada has been active in Clayoquot Sound for decades because of the highly productive salmonid populations and their importance to the local fishing industry.

• The Federal Department of Indian and Northern Affairs is quite active in the region, given the number of First Nations communities and their isolation from many resources and social services.

ECONOMIC COUNCILS

• The Council of Forestry Industries and the B.C. Forest Alliance are both very active and well-funded in expressing the positions of the logging corporations.

• The ecotourism organizations are small and poorly organized.

NATIONALLY- AND GLOBALLY-ORIENTED ENVIRONMENTAL GROUPS

• Aside from FOCS, the Western Canada Wilderness Committee (WCWC) has the longest history of working for conservation in the area, of supporting the Nuu-chah-nulth in conservation, and of developing cooperative projects. WCWC did not formerly participate or support the civil disobedience movement at Kennedy River Bridge.

• Ecotrust is a small Portland, Oregon-based conservation foundation concerned with the conservation of temperate rainforest, and which in recent years has supported the Nuu-chah-nulth in several innovative conservation projects.

• Greenpeace has been active in Clayoquot in recent years and members of both its B.C. and its international branches were involved in the Peace Camp.

• The Temperate Rain Forest Alliance is a small group based in Vancouver.

• The Natural Resources Defense Fund is a Washington D.C. organization which has been increasingly involved in the conservation of rainforest in cooperation with local indigenous communities.

• The Sierra Club (of Western Canada and the U.S.) has been very active in the conservation of temperate rainforest on Vancouver Island for two decades and has compiled some of the most comprehensive reports on the status of the island's forests.

These groups, along with the Friends of Clayoquot Sound, have played a crucial role in alerting the public to the dangers of clearcutting in Clayoquot Sound. They depend, however, on private donations, and have had difficulty in competing with the large corporations, aided as they are by the provincial government.


## VII.    The False Compromise of the April 1993 Cabinet Decision and the Abuse of Science

The April 1993 "compromise" on Clayoquot Sound by the British Columbia Cabinet was based on insufficient inventory and ecological data. Put simply, the Clayoquot Land Use Decision cannot ensure the maintenance of biological diversity or full representation of ancient temperate forest ecosystems. The links between data and decision-making were either undocumented or unclear. While it is true that subsequent forest land-use policy changes were introduced, these changes have not yet had a measurable effect on lessening the rate of the liquidation of the old-growth forest ecosystems, particularly for those with "big trees" and higher accumulations of standing biomass, for it is these big trees that prove so attractive and profitable to the logging companies. Optimistic estimates for actual implementation of the new practices "on the ground" suggest that it will take another two to three years.[61] By this time, a substantial portion of the most crucial lowland ancient forest in Clayoquot Sound will have been liquidated.

Even with a reduction in the annual allowable cut on Vancouver Island, the pressures for rapid liquidation of the ancient forests of Clayoquot Sound remain strong. The lack of scientific basis for the April 1993 decision works counter to the efforts of the international Biosphere Reserves network for better use of inventory data[62] in land-use decision-making as well as Canada's participation in the *Convention on Biological Diversity*.[63]

The Cabinet of the Government of British Columbia acquiesced to a plan largely developed by bureaucracies formed by the previous Social Credit Party government. When compared to most other contemporary efforts to preserve primary forest (even those in the tropics of the Third World), the body of research on the area's biological diversity, landscape ecology, and conservation requirements can be seen to be inadequate. At the species level, there was a relatively complete level of inventory of vertebrates and vascular plants. At the subspecies level and the distributions of rarer vascular plants, there are, however, gaps. Moreover, for terrestrial invertebrates and non-vascular plants, particularly those associated with the canopies of mature forest ecosystems and marine invertebrates, there are large holes in our knowledge.

At the various levels of ecosystems, communities, and regional landscape processes, there have been no adequate inventories of old-growth, although a major effort began with the Ministry of Forest's Old-Growth Strategy Task Force in 1990. A better classification system of "mature"coastal western hemlock forest ecosystems (with an emphasis on discerning a range of processes and attributes related to forest age, soil, and landform; along with maps with precision of 1:20,000 or finer) is still several years away. There are even major problems with the current Ministry of Forests Inventory Branch "Forest Cover" maps. These forest cover maps are inadequate as a basis for planning for reserves fully representative of old-growth ecosystems. They currently indicate only a small number of information categories needed to make conservation decisions—such as the history of timber cutting, the younger age classes of forest, and vague aggregations of the mature classes of forest.

The information available to those involved in the April 13th land-use Decision was minimal. There had been only two brief summaries of the knowledge of the biological diversity[64] and landscape processes of Clayoquot Sound—as part of the unsuccessful efforts for a "strategy[65] for sustainable development"[66]—and that compilation was not intended to highlight the *gaps* in knowledge. The assessments of Vancouver Island landscapes and their fragmentation from large-scale clearcut logging has indicated only a small number of "intact" unlogged watersheds and large contiguous lowland old-growth forest. But even these assessments have not been at an adequate level of precision for making decisions about "integrated resource management" within these remaining wilderness areas.[67] There is no indication of any other major studies on the biological diversity of the Clayoquot Sound area that had been conducted and disseminated on or before January 1993, when the current "compromise option" was developed by Mr. Robert Prescott-Allen[68] and the Port Alberni Regional Office of the B.C. Ministry of Forests.

Given that the information for a proper decision was lacking, it is no surprise to find that the plan itself is flawed. The easiest way of seeing the flaws is to consider first the three different classifications used to divide up Clayoquot Sound, and then to examine their characteristics. The three classifications are 1. Protected Areas; 2. General Integrated Management Areas; 3. Special Management Areas.

## 1. PROTECTED AREAS

• There are some previously established protected areas, such as the heavily-used Long Beach area of Pacific Rim National Park and a large portion of the relatively intact forest of the badly managed Strathcona Provincial Park. There were also a few small provincial parks.

• The eventual management framework for the new protected areas, created in the April 1993 decision, is still unresolved. At least some areas will become part of the provincial park system.

## 2. GENERAL INTEGRATED MANAGEMENT AREAS

• These areas were misleadingly coloured green in the government publication and are to be cut, very quickly, using conventional clearcut logging practices.[69]

## 3. SPECIAL MANAGEMENT AREAS

• There are a small number of Recreation areas where some logging will be allowed.

• There are a small number of Wildlife management areas with some logging.

• Most of the Special Management Areas are Scenic Corridors with intensive pressures for liquidation of ancient forest along with protection of some visual values,[70] which may prove to be largely an exercise in bad cosmetics.

• Lands "Not Included in Decision," such as Meares Island, because of other unresolved legal aspects of aboriginal title.

THE PROTECTED AREAS IN THE APRIL 1993 DECISION AND
THEIR LACK OF LONG-TERM VIABILITY FOR CONSERVATION OF
BIOLOGICAL DIVERSITY

In the 48,500 hectares of "Protected Areas" that were delineated
in and subsequently removed from possibilities for logging in the
April 1993 decision,[71] there has been no formal analysis of the viability of, or the requirements for management[72] for, conservation of biological diversity. The scientific and management
rationales for their designs have never been made clear. In fact,
we are left with a series of problematic fragments in an already
highly fragmented natural landscape. These tracts, while often
lovely and interesting, are "scraps" of land. Moreover, they were
never under much industrial threat anyway, since they had no
value for resource extraction. A further irony is that, although
they were not particularly threatened before the decision, they
are now under increasing threat—even as gazetted protected
areas—because they are adjacent to what will be potentially dam-
aging industrial operations. The reason is that there has been little coordination with the adjacent areas designated for industrial
use, and the borders have had no regulations imposed. The following presents a list of the "scraps" that allowed the Cabinet of
British Columbia to call the Clayoquot Land Use Decision a
"compromise":

- one large contiguous watershed adjacent to
  Strathcona Provincial Park, the Megin River Basin,
  surrounded by a large area on the outside of the
  Clayoquot planning unit that is under pressure for
  clearcut logging (plus some Integrated
  Management Area and Recreation Special
  Management Areas);
- one entire island in Shelter Inlet, Obstruction
  Island;
- a portion of the shore of Sidney Inlet, surrounded
  by General Integrated Management areas and
  Scenic Corridor and Recreation Special

Management areas slated for intensive logging;

- a narrow shore strip along Hesquiat Harbour, mainly buffered with Scenic Corridor that could still involve intensive logging;
- a tiny park at Hesquiat Lake, surrounded by Scenic Corridor and Integrated Management Area that could still involve intensive logging;
- the southern and western portions of Hesquiat Peninsula along the shores but with an upland core of Integrated Management Area which could still involve intensive logging;
- a strip along the west coast of Flores Island, adjacent to Scenic Corridor and some Integrated Management Area;
- a strip along the west coast of Vargas Island, adjacent to Scenic Corridor and some Integrated Management Area;
- the island off the west coast of Vargas Island, Blunden Island;
- the tiny Dunlap and Morfee Islands;
- a small park at Dawley Passage with the Lane Islet which is adjacent to Scenic Corridor;
- the tiny Kennedy River Bog surrounded by Integrated Management Area and Scenic Corridor;
- two miniscule strips near the small park already established at the south end of Kennedy Lake, adjacent to Scenic Corridor and Integrated Management Area;
- the small area around the Tranquil Creek headwaters, completely surrounded by Integrated Management Area;
- the shore on the west side of Clayoquot Arm and the lower valley of the Clayoquot River basin, nearly completely surrounded by General Integrated Management area and adjacent to some Scenic Corridor; and

- the Clayoquot Plateau, almost completely surrounded by General Integrated Management Area
  and adjacent to some Scenic Corridor.

The striking feature of the ecosystems of these protected areas is the small percentage of their total area that has highly productive lowland forest with large accumulations of standing biomass.

What is lacking in the *new protected areas* is the type of old-growth forest that is attractive for timber harvesting—with large trees—and which has been the least inventoried in terms of ecosystem processes and respective biological resources. It is these types of highly complex habitats that support a myriad of only partially documented invertebrates and non-vascular and vascular plants. The only large, contiguous protected area with these kinds of ancient forest ecosystems in the "compromise" is the Megin. Most of the larger protected areas, such as the Hesquiat protected area, the Flores protection strip, the Vargas protection strip, and the Clayoquot Plateau preserve comprise relatively old bog ecosystems with limited accumulation of surface biomass.[73]

The second striking feature of the protected areas is that island ecosystems with relatively intact mosaics of old-growth and terrestrial marine interface zones are virtually absent. Like the forests of Clayoquot, these forest/marine interface ecosystems have global significance. Under the April 1993 decision, the majority of Flores and half of Vargas Island are to be intensively harvested for timber. Of the 14 smaller islands that are considered in the April 1993 decision, only the largest, Obstruction, plus the three near Maquinna Park—Blunden, Dunlap, and Morfee—are protected. The other small islands are nearly all in Scenic Corridor where clearcut logging is still very much a possibility.

The third feature of the protected areas is that they include only modest protection of sheltered bodies of marine areas and their respective shores. Yet there is continued pressure to use these waters for industrial activities such as log dumps. Estuaries were particularly neglected in the April 1993 decision. A large number of them are in the Scenic Corridors, where logging can continue. Of the larger estuaries, only two will be fully protected, with two others only partially secure from degradation.

A fourth characterization of the protected areas established in the April 1993 decision is that they will become a highly fragmented "dog's breakfast" of narrow strips, dominated by degraded areas of logging. There will be much less biotic connectivity than at the present time. In ecological terms, these natural islands and habitat fragments will be cast further adrift under increasing pressure from local recreation and international tourism. In order to maintain natural linkages and flows, there will need to be corridors established in both the Integrated Management Areas and the Scenic Corridors. So far, there have been no substantive initiatives on the part of the Province of B.C. to manage the Scenic Corridors so as to maintain connectivity and biological diversity. Even in the recent versions of environmental assessment legislation, no consideration has been given to the use of an environmental impact review framework to determine and mitigate the potential negative influences of the additional industrial operations on the natural areas established under the April 1993 decision.

THE FATE OF ANCIENT FORESTS IN THE GENERAL INTEGRATED MANAGEMENT AND SPECIAL MANAGEMENT AREAS

After having examined the "Protected Areas," we can now turn to both the "General Integrated Management Areas" and the "Special Management Areas." The reason for treating the two categories together is quite simply that logging is allowed in both. And in both areas, the April "compromise" contains no protection of the ancient forest and shore ecosystems and the biological diversity of Clayoquot Sound. In fact, there will be no possibility of preserving the large trees in these areas until a number of conditions are met. First, the Scientific Panel (established in October 1993 after many people voiced their concerns about the fate of the large trees) must make its final recommendations, and these must be fully implemented. Second, the new Forestry Practices Guide must be brought into law, fully enforced and guided by rational criteria. This proviso is crucial, because at the moment the Code says virtually nothing about enforcement. Third, there must be formal mechanisms to integrate requirements for protection of biological diversity in the Scenic Corridors. Fourth, the protected area systems must be redesigned to represent the full range of old-growth, island, and shore ecosystems. Until these conditions are met, timber harvesting activities will continue to destroy these biological resources, as well as to fragment and degrade all of the ecosystems of Clayoquot Sound.

It is in the Special Management Areas, especially along shores and in lowlands, where considerable timber harvesting has already taken place and where there are some of the greatest pressures for cutting because of accessibility and high timber values. The General Integrated Management areas comprise 44.7% of the Clayoquot Sound planning area, while the Special Management Areas comprise another 17.6%.[74]

If we turn now to look at the present on-going logging of Clayoquot Sound, such as described later in this book by Christopher Hatch, we can see that the rate of cutting of ancient forest in the Clayoquot Sound area has probably not declined significantly since April 1993. The April 1993 decision embodied a commitment to harvest levels of between 400,000 and 600,000 cubic metres per year which, though lower than the 800,000 to 900,000 cubic metres originally proposed by industry for annual cutting, amounts to one of the most rapid levels of clearcut logging for any similar region in the history of British Columbia, not to mention North America. The reality is that the rate of cutting in 1993 and 1994[75] could well be the most rapid ever in Clayoquot Sound. Moreover, the ecological impacts will be compounded by the fact that the area's second-growth timber, from logging in earlier decades, is not yet mature. This puts particularly severe pressures on the remaining ancient forest ecosystems with highly valuable timber in lowland areas—particularly along shores and in valley bottoms. Moreover, the mills of Port Alberni require large numbers of trees on a daily basis, and the only way to maintain the mills' efficiency is to cut intensively the ancient forests of Clayoquot. As a result, the remaining landscapes of primary forests will be so heavily fragmented that the ecosystems in large portions of Clayoquot Sound will be effectively liquidated.

What would happen if clearcut logging operations were curtailed in Clayoquot Sound? The alternative practices would involve the cutting of fewer trees per area, over longer rotations and with a greater number of entries. The total wood output would decline in the short-term in favour of a secure long-term production. Any "conversion" to ecosystem-based approaches to harvesting and silviculture would require new equipment and training of the labour force. Any ecosystem-based system would require "patchiness" and more ongoing cutting at lower levels, which could involve risks of environmental problems of their own. But these problems could probably be better managed than those of clearcutting. Yet even if new approaches to harvesting are introduced, it needs to be emphasized that certain standing aspects of the ancient forests must always be present in sufficient quantities for the ecosystem to be maintained. In other words, without clear criteria for "new forestry,"[76] even the "new" practices could still degrade the old-growth forest ecosystems, transforming them into plantations. In the process, an increasing portion of the land base would also become less productive because of engineering failures and erosion.

When one looks at the landscapes of Clayoquot in relation to the rest of Vancouver Island, another problem with logging becomes evident. The entire island has been overcut over the last two decades. A decrease in cutting and a downsizing is now inevitable, as was proposed by the Commission on Resources and Environment in February 1994.[77] But even if cutting declines and practices become more ecosystem-based[78] in other parts of Vancouver Island, this will not diminish the pressure on Clayoquot Sound. Given the industrial apparatus that is already in place in such communities as Port Alberni and Ucluelet for the intensive processing of large trees, the opposite is more likely. Clayoquot Sound has become the sacrifice by the Cabinet of B.C. to the old order. The CORE recommendations for the rest of Vancouver Island could actually be used to continue to push levels of timber-removal in Clayoquot Sound well above the thresholds of sustainability in terms of both natural carrying capacities and the habitat requirements for persistence of local biological diversity.

As should be evident, the "technical difficulties"—from lack of time, studies, trained personnel, and funding, and the anti-conservation biases within the provincial government—represent a land management bureaucracy in crisis. The April 1993 decision was the last major land-use planning decision in British Columbia to use the old frameworks—ones that were grossly biased towards extraction of raw resources over other social benefits. In effect, the 1993 conflict over Clayoquot turns out to have been a move from older forms of blatant neocolonialism to newer forms of over-exploitation of the land and First Nations communities that are only a little less obvious.

## VIII. International Standards

As was mentioned earlier, it is possible for the governments of British Columbia, Canada, and the Nuu-chah-nulth nation to make a formal proposal that Clayoquot Sound become a Biosphere Reserve.[79] The protected areas in the April 1993 decision would become the cores, with the Special Management Areas the buffers, and the Integrated Management Areas as the transition zones. Yet such a scenario—while it looks positive—actually negates the spirit of the Biosphere Reserve concept. The reason is that the international Biosphere committees have called for better inventorying *before* major land-use activities in buffers and transition zones take place. As has been seen, this inventorying has not yet taken place.

On its side, the government of British Columbia has suggested that the April 1993 decision would contribute to Canada's obligations[80] under the *Convention on Biological Diversity*. Again, however, the problems with the design of the protected areas and the extent, speed, and questionable legality of the current cutting operations[81] suggest that the opposite is more the case. Article 7 of the Clayoquot Land Use Decision, titled "Identification and Monitoring," talks of the need to understand the components of biological diversity. But there has simply not been sufficient inventorying of specific aspects of the old-growth forest ecosystems in this area, in terms of attributes and processes. Nor has there been adequate ecological mapping.

The government of British Columbia also points to Article 8 of the Clayoquot Land Use Decision, titled "In-situ Conservation," as promoting Canada's obligations on biological diversity. Article 8 of the Clayoquot Land Use Decision, refers to the establishment of "a system of protected areas or areas where special measures need to be taken to conserve biological diversity." But Article 8 also suggests the establishment of guidelines for selection of protected areas for the conservation of biological diversity and for "maintenance of viable populations." There would also be promotion of "environmentally sound and sustainable development in areas adjacent to protected areas." So far, however, these things have yet to be established for Clayoquot Sound. Similarly, Point 8.1 involves a commitment to regulation and management of "significant adverse effects on biological diversity," but it will take at least two to three years to put such frameworks in place for Clayoquot Sound.

Once one looks at the kind of planning that has been used for Clayoquot Sound, one realizes that the criteria are hopelessly outdated in terms of what is now being practised and demanded in the international community. Much of early 20th-century nature conservation was preoccupied with variations on the largely nineteenth-century colonial notion of the national park. In the current period, with its tremendous rates of loss of habitat and degradation of regional environments, the pool of interventions available to the planner and manager has been expanded. The underlying relationships and possibilities have been further explored.

It will be useful here to pause for a brief moment to outline the sorts of international criteria that need to be applied to Clayoquot Sound. The following material is somewhat theoretical, but it is important to state publicly the principles essential to future planning for all regions such as Clayoquot Sound.

The tenets of the emerging theory of environmental planning for the conservation of biological diversity involve a myriad of interventions. Such measures are grouped into the following:

1.  protected area allocation;
2.  reserve management; and
3.  regulation of land-use in external areas.

Three sets of trade-offs emerge, related to requirements for maintenance of biological diversity in networks of protected habitat across districts and regions:

1.  between area of habitat protection and regulation;
2.  between total area in reserves and the quality of
    that habitat;
3.  between management within protected areas and
    regulation outside of reserves to mitigate impacts of
    regional degradation.

The resulting conservation possibilities vary with the different contexts. They reflect intrinsic biological requirements and ecosystem structures as well as historical, institutional, and cultural factors. The highlighting of relationships between certain factors and constraints for habitat protection and some expansion in land-use, can support identification of more precise and viable strategies for conservation across districts and regions.

The following are various questions that should be first outlined as the basis for any modern conservation effort:

- definitions of criteria for conservation and development;
- the setting of socially acceptable levels of risk and security by the full set of "user" groups and stakeholders;
- assessment of local biological diversity and reviews of the gaps in inventorying;
- the recognition of the island biogeography dynamics as related to reserve size and isolation;
- interpretation of the SLOSS (single large or several small reserves)
- debates for particular environments and ecosystems;
- strategies to minimize fragmentation of habitat in terms of management of various natural and human-induced processes related to specific ecosystems and habitats; and
- the setting of minimum requirements as a basis for reserve design including population size, number of populations, population demographics, intraspecific variation, and diversity in terms of specific genotypes, habitat features and respective sites, diversity of biophysical conditions, and the nature of landscape mosaics and patterns of disturbance.

The notion of the network for habitat protection also needs to be clarified for particular settings. The metaphor of the reserve as an island has given way to that of the boundary of a reserve as part of constellations of concentric "membranes" and edges. Such filters are highly sensitive to the interplay of external and internal forces. For example, in a discussion of national parks in Italy, there was a shift from protected areas as "protectionist instruments" to "elements of total planning"[82] in open systems. It had become apparent to the Italians that any "attempts to create or operate on a park while considering it as a closed system are destined to failure." The notion of a park as an island, somehow immune to the impacts of the surrounding clearcuts, was applied in the April 1993 decision for Clayoquot, and if we are to judge from what has occurred subsequently in the protests, the idea is doomed to failure.

The modern rationales for active management of protected areas emerged with the awareness that few of the national parks in the United States were sufficiently large to be self-regulatory ecological units. This biological concept was expanded by Pyle when he stated:

> The fewer and less intense the hostile pressure from outside the reserves, the larger the area set aside, the lower the number of visitors and the friendlier the social climate in which the reserve exists, the greater its defensibility and manageability.[83]

As is apparent, the 1993 Clayoquot decision allowed for only one relatively large protected area of the kind described by Pyle: the Megin River watershed. As a result, future management of the Clayoquot area—with its many strips and corridors and patchworks of clearcuts—will almost certainly prove very expensive to manage. These high management expenses will shift yet another financial burden onto future generations.

The emerging science of landscape ecology[84] may provide a sufficiently rigorous theoretical framework to begin to manage cumulative impacts through focusing on spatial indices with measurable properties. Such landscape approaches to wildlife and ecosystem management may constitute the beginnings of a vocabulary to manage spatial relationships involving:

- *cores* of relatively unaltered habitat (aside from some traditional Nuu-chah-nulth uses), with careful management of (eco)tourism, and procurement of samples of wild species with genetic resources;

- *buffers* with highly regulated activities including traditional Nuu-chah-nulth uses, the bulk of tourism, some highly regulated timber harvesting, and some roads;

- *corridors* that are sufficiently wide to allow for connectivity for prescribed species; and

- *barriers* to invasions of alien species which, so far, have not been a major problem in the area.

The applications of these conservation concepts may vary radically with landscape structure, biogeography and the choice of indicator species.

Sets of biodiversity indicators could function, therefore, to guide the choice of habitats, sites and indefinite and prescribed conditions for the best formalization of these functional categories of conservation. The composition of suits of indicators should vary in terms of conservation criteria, perceived threats to biological diversity, and the interpretation of principles of landscape ecology. Such indicators,[85] involving attributes, habitat features, disturbance factors and species, can be identified, and measures can be more precisely established for ongoing "adaptive management."[86] Modern alterations of island forests are producing changes which are often not comparable to those of natural processes or impacts from traditional societies. Urbanization and tourist development, for example, can obliterate shore ecosystems and create barriers with negative impacts. These dangers are clearly increasing in the Clayoquot, where more and more visitors come every year. Moreover, because the scales[87] and rates of modern change are often very great, the tracts of primary forest that remain are often degraded on an indefinite basis due to expansion of edges and decreasing size of habitat units. The size, shapes and formation patterns of patches and gaps within successional mosaics is particularly central in determining the sensitivity to fragmentation of particular archipelagoes. Similarly, there are variable regimens of disturbance and ecotones which enter into the equation of intrinsic vulnerability of loss of species from fragmentation.

Little of the research so far has provided an institutional basis for *construction* of more comprehensive frameworks of decision-making. There have been two principal obstacles. The first has been the lack of comprehensive methods for identification of indicators[88] of conservation of local biological diversity and for the persistence of vulnerable elements under particular regimens of habitat protection. A second obstacle has been the lack of a theory for the spatial and functional processes which are the prerequisites for an applied landscape ecology for biodiversity conservation.[89] The key information links between landscape ecology and conservation planning require spatial models with natural and social variables.

Rarely can or should natural areas be protected solely because of a requirement for maintenance of local biological diversity. There are usually additional "environmental" concerns, such as the need for continued levels of production of certain species important for subsistence or as commodities, and there are other non-market values related to recreation, heritage, and visual resources. Yet there have been few discussions on the identification of the gaps[90] in the systems of protected areas, in terms of conservation of biological diversity. Similarly, there are few theoretical discussions of the integration of an expanding array of noncommodity values into more comprehensive landscape planning. Even within ecological reserves and national parks, there is the issue of multiple use—even when just confined to balancing pressures for "nonconsumptive ecotourism" and new technological activities, such as preservation of genetic resources.[91] Therefore, particular conservation measures are never fully comprehensive and tend to favour and be more effective for the maintenance of some biological resources, with certain purposes and levels of security, than others.

The April 1993 Land Use Decision simply cannot be adapted with additional data and tinkering to comply with international standards for conservation of biodiversity. The entire framework of reductionist science that was employed, often cynically, must be expanded and rethought. To attempt to repackage the April 1993 plan into a UNESCO-recognized biosphere reserve would be another insult to the area and another misuse of science.

## IX.   Changes in land-use Policy in Clayoquot Sound Subsequent to April 1993

Since the April 1993 decision, there have been few new efforts to improve upon the inventory of the biological resources of the area. As the climate of conflict has intensified, resources for this research (unless under the rubric of the April 1993[92] decision) have dwindled. So far, little if any of the provincial money promised under the Interim Measures Agreement has been allocated for new biodiversity and (Nuu-chah-nulth) ethnobiology research and inventories. It is true that changes in forest practices for the area were announced in June 1993.[93] As well, both the Provincial Forester and the Commission on Resources and Environment recommended, in early 1994, a reduction in future cutting of ancient forest on Vancouver Island, largely because of overcutting in the past two decades. But neither of these recommendations will influence cutting rates in Clayoquot Sound for at least another year. Moreover, even if these reforms were fully implemented, they would mean only a greater level of fragmentatation, only a slowing of the liquidation of the old-growth forest ecosystems in Clayoquot.

The Forest Practices Code[94] for British Columbia forests was proposed and is expected to be made into law in the fall of 1994. While it represents a positive step, it will not be fully implemented for at least several years, and in the meantime a number of interim reports have been released that confirm the public's fears about the kind and extent of active logging at the present time.

In looking to the future, one can see that the May 10, 1994, _Progress Report_ 2 of the Scientific Panel[95] provides some important new opportunities for conservation in Clayoquot Sound. This report has not received the wide-spread discussion that it deserves, perhaps because the Panel's final report is still awaited. Nevertheless, the report offers an important change in perspective on the way that Clayoquot Sound is to be handled in future, and I wish to point to some of its most important features.

IMPORTANT RECOMMENDATIONS

- *"Current planning procedures are inadequate for sustainable ecosystem management. The Panel recommends that planning in Clayoquot Sound be ecosystem-based and multidisciplinary; it should integrate the full spectrum of resource values. The Panel further recommends that planning be conducted at ecologically relevant time and spatial scales"* (page 2). The implications of this statement, in the context of the Interim Measures Agreement, is that the April 1993 decisions and map delineations should be cancelled. To replace them, a planning process centred on Nuu-chah-nulth communities and the requirements for maintenance and conservation of a range of biological resources needs to be quickly developed.

- *"Care is required in undeveloped watersheds. The Panel recommends delaying activity in undeveloped watersheds until adequate inventories are prepared, exemplary forest practices and silvicultural systems demonstrated elsewhere can be applied, and a prequalification procedure is in place"* (page 2). This requirement for a delay in any industrial activity in the undeveloped watersheds was the major point of the people who demonstrated at the blockades. That a government-supported panel came to the same conclusion indicates that the protestors were correct in wanting to "delay" the building of roads and the logging. In effect, the Panel's finding calls into question the whole April 1993 decision and the credibility of the present provincial cabinet. More problematic is the reality that logging interests cannot afford to wait, that the Interim Measures Agreement gives Nuu-chah-nulth communities only partial rights to decide when and where logging can occur. There is not yet a functioning mechanism for the Nuu-chah-nulth and the Province of B.C. to determine when logging is appropriate in "undeveloped" watersheds. Given the global significance of the area as a baseline, it is evident that little, if any, extraction of old-growth timber should be allowed in these watersheds[96]—as long as economic alternatives for the Nuu-chah-nulth can be created.

• *"These changes are major, and the Panel recommends an imple-mentation plan be established and publicized for those steps requiring sig-nificant time to implement"* (page 2). It is crucial for the conservation organizations to support and disseminate this rec-ommendation and to pressure the Province of British Columbia into a swift implementation. Otherwise, implementation could drag on for years while substantially more of the areas with rela-tively intact ecosystems are clearcut. Given that the recommen-dations of the Panel have no "teeth," it may take the threat of a continued and expanded boycott, from both Europe and the U.S., for a conservation planning framework controlled by the Nuu-chah-nulth, to come into being in the coming years.

• Recommendation 2.3.2 (page 11) is particularly crucial and contentious. It calls for setting desired levels of *"goods and services to be produced from Clayoquot Sound (e.g., cubic metres of wood, visitor days) through a comprehensive ecosystem assessment and planning process."* This is not purely a technical exercise, as it may seem at first sight, since it involves numerous questions of social equity and distribution of costs and benefits. The role of the conserva-tion organizations in the construction of such highly politicized models of goods and services output can be to advocate—

1. that the various Nuu-chah-nulth communities and sectors are fully considered in fair distribution of "goods and services" and environmental costs and benefits;

2. that a balanced and secure shift to sustainable livelihoods is the basis for economic development for the Nuu-chah-nulth communities while assuring jobs for the largest portion possible of the area's non-native populations; and

3. that the global significance of these relatively intact ancient forest and terrestrial-marine ecosystems, in terms of research and education, be considered, and the risk standards for minimizing loss of re-

sources and degradation of ecosystems be adequate.

- *"Broaden the silvicultural systems used in Clayoquot Sound, beyond clearcutting. Select appropriate silvicultural systems to maintain natural landscape patterns and stand structures, and to meet a variety of management of objectives other than timber production"* (page 12). This is the most understated point in the entire document. But "broaden" still suggests allowing some, if not a great deal of, clearcutting. The conservation organizations should continue to argue against the removal of trees from old-growth forest ecosystems until the new "systems" that maintain full sets of respective ecosystem processes are fully established. If the government spends three years to develop these approaches while continuing with the current logging practices, much of the ancient ecosystems of Clayoquot Sound will be lost.

- *"Establish appropriate phase-in periods for standards requiring major changes to current practices. This will allow stakeholders time to adjust and will help to ensure compliance"* (page 12). It is crucial that the new conservation campaigns work to pressure the Government of British Columbia to support making this "phase-in period" as rapid as possible, while minimizing short-term economic losses to Nuu-chah-nulth and non-native communities. One must not forget that, for the transition to "sustainability," there is still considerably more support available for non-native timber-industry workers and enterprises than there is for Nuu-chah-nulth economic development.

As is evident, the recommendations of the Scientific Panel—even in its interim reports—promise much. Until the final recommendations are made, however, little can be done. Even then, the main problem will be with implementation, for the recommendations fly in the face of current practices.

## X. Resolving Conflicts over Facts, Notions, Constructs, and Values

While a full understanding of the underlying dynamics of the Clayoquot conflict would require a review of the last 200 years of history in British Columbia, it has become apparent that the key to viable alternatives to the present conflict lies in the development of political, social and administrative mechanisms to reflect public concerns. The following is a "laundry list" of perspectives and interpretations that need to be clarified:

### BIOPHYSICAL / "HARD" SCIENCE

• More specific definitions of "old-growth" forest are needed, with specific types of ancient forest ecosystems delineated.

• The full extent of local biological diversity needs to be considered for particular areas, including the filling of information gaps for vascular and non-vascular plants, vertebrates and invertebrates.

• The key ecological processes (at various scales across time and space), and the landscape ecology of particular areas need to be identified.

• The vulnerability to fragmentation of forested landscapes targeted for industrial logging needs to be considered at every level of land-use planning.

• More specific standards related to soil erosion, mass wasting, fisheries dynamics, and habitat quality are needed.

• The margins of risks and thresholds related to change and environmental degradation must be set in a manner that allows for more public discussion.

### SOCIAL SCIENCES

• The historical basis of the current claims of First Nations groups in terms of natural resources, territory, and sovereignty must be much more fully recognized.

• The statistics on employment and unemployment trends and the roles of such factors as automation in the forest industry must be more fully discussed in public.

• There are numerous ethics and divergent sets of perceptions at work in the public's view of the remaining areas with large tracts of old-growth forest. A much wider perspective on these views must be developed if our society is going to evolve beyond the simplistic dichotomy of "jobs versus preservation."

• Strategies for coping with and thriving in the global marketplace must be developed. It is necessary to identify a range of approaches to economic development, with various costs and benefits to particular communities and social groups. The current strategies of the large logging companies and the Government of British Columbia are narrow and unworkable.

• The nature of trends in tourist demand must be more carefully explored.

• The approach of the Government of British Columbia to "visual resources management"[97] is still remarkably reductionist and limited to a small number of scenic values and viewing groups. Cosmetic attempts to hide clearcuts with fringes simply do not work.

• Conservation of biological diversity in particular areas is needed along with the determination of minimum objectives to maintain corridors.

• Alternatives to clearcutting need to be identified. The appropriateness of "new forestry" practices determined for particular ecological zones, sites, and operating conditions need to be considered.

• The concepts of and means for mediation, consensus, and democratic decision-making, recognizing the different stakes and respective groups, must be expanded.

## XI.   *Epiloque to the 1993 Demonstrations*

If the biological diversity and ancient forest ecosystems of

Clayoquot Sound are to be protected, it is necessary to implement quickly the following recommendations. If these actions are not initiated, it is highly likely that significant elements of biological diversity and ancient forest ecosystem processes will be jeopardized in the coming three years:

1.  The protected areas must be expanded and re-designed to better represent old-growth forest ecosystems, intact island/rainforest ecosystems, estuarine and shore ecosystems. The protected areas must be expanded and redesigned to better function as a network with enhanced connectivity.

2.  The highest priorities for management of the Scenic Corridors must still be maintenance of the local biological diversity, old-growth forest attributes, and ecosystem processes. The protection of visual, recreation, and heritage resources is of secondary importance, after which should come possibilities for removal of some timber.

3.  Decisions on timber harvesting, especially in the "Integrated Management Zone," should be derived from a fuller classification system of the remaining old-growth ecosystems based on key attributes and processes with options identified to maintain them.

4.  All decisions on new timber harvesting in Clayoquot Sound should be deferred until completion of detailed mapping of traditional-use areas of the Nuu-chah-nulth. If logging continues in the areas that are identified, even greater cuts in the level of timber cutting may well be necessary in order to compensate holders of traditional title and rights in terms of specific resources.

5. The Joint Management Board outlined in the Interim Measures Agreement should be made as independent of government and industry as possible, and should be supported in the coordinating and evaluating of research related to inventories, landscape processes, human ecology, impact assessments, reserve designs, and logging practices.

6. An international monitoring group is also necessary, especially for the review of the Total Resource Plans outlined in the Interim Measures Agreement.[98] It can be composed of independent experts and should exist for at least three years. Such a monitoring group could track the cutting and its impacts as well as propose revised reserve designs and new cutting permits. It could also debate land management prescriptions. The international monitoring group should be organized to:

   a) minimize conflicts of interest;
   b) be oriented to advising Nuu-chah-nulth communities who own particular territories and ecosystems;
   c) be separate from any provincial and federal government, as well as international agencies; and
   d) provide and disseminate credible and current information on the state of ecosystems and land management in Clayoquot Sound.

## XII. Principles of Support for the Nuu-Chah-Nulth Conservation Efforts

The Nuu-chah-nulth communities of Clayoquot Sound have various historical relationships to conservation movements and initiatives. They also have traditional tenure and stewardship of their lands, which includes logging and the need for increased jobs and services. Conservation organizations must be prepared to listen and work with particular communities, sectors, and groups for a protracted period. No matter what forms of joint management develop, the major question in native communities in Clayoquot Sound remains: Who is really committed to staying and working within the emerging frameworks of the Interim Measures Agreement? And who are more like tourists? Without increased contact, information, jobs, and other kinds of tangible "support," it will prove impossible to form and maintain the kinds of long-term "conservation partnerships" that can counter the pressures and enticements of the logging companies.

To assume that there will be an automatic improvement in conservation after the Interim Measures Agreement, would be to ignore both the history of poor treatment meted out to the Nuu-chah-nulth communities and their present state of under-development. After basic social services become available—services similar to those in the rest of southern Canada—perhaps there can be a basis for talking about better conservation. The Nuu-chah-nulth will need unqualified support to develop and carry-out conservation that contributes to *their* development, defined on *their* own terms. This will require years of personal contact and exchanges of information, all within the priorities of particular Nuu-chah-nulth communities. The following are some principles for supporting community-based conservation initiatives in Clayoquot Sound:

• Each of the Nuu-chah-nulth communities has different needs and perspectives and may often have differing priorities for conservation and development. While conservation scientists and advocates must take great care not to be divisive, it is equally important to work with each Nuu-chah-nulth community on its own terms, and to link programmes across Clayoquot Sound only after the programmes have been initiated by specific Nuu-chah-nulth communities and groups.

• Outside scientists and environmentalists from other parts of Vancouver Island and elsewhere must spend considerable time *listening and learning* about traditional land management[99] before they will be able to support fully the conservation initiatives of these communities.

• Particular Nuu-chah-nulth communities may choose to develop their linkages with various local, bio-regional, national, North American, and overseas organizations. Unconditional support from "environmental" groups is necessary. The environmental groups will develop successful alliances with Nuu-chah-nulth communities when they contribute to decolonization of Clayoquot Sound and are not perceived as part of any recolonization processes.

## XIII.   Conclusion

Having spent considerable time describing and analyzing Clayoquot Sound's ecology of conflict—in ideas, ethics, values, economic realities, and peoples' lives—I wish to return to a central point that must not be forgotten: Clayoquot Sound is still being logged—even as I write—with practices that have been banned in much of the world. If the "ecology of conflict" of the last few years has had a redeeming lesson, it is to teach us that we need to understand more of the underlying relationships among stakeholders, ideas, global market forces, and place. Once this is achieved, we will be in a position to transform the conflict into an increasingly global movement that supports the Nuu-chah-nulth in their long struggle to take back authentic stewardship of their lands and waters. Vancouver Island and the world have changed a great deal since the beginning of the struggle for conservation and sustainable development in Clayoquot Sound. It remains to be seen whether the Interim Measures Agreement between the Nuu-chah-nulth and the Government of British Columbia is little more than "a pact of semi-colonization."[100] Through the efforts of those participating in the 1993 blockades, Clayoquot is now a testing ground, a place of learning, for the development of authentic alliances and exchanges—part of our efforts to build democracy and freedom of inquiry on the Pacific Coast of Canada. How well we do this will determine many aspects of our lives and communities for many years to come.

\* \* \*

This essay is dedicated to the memory of my father and his neighbour, Chief Christopher Paul. Ross Sheldon Ingram (1905-1971) was born in Kitsilano and worked in industrial operations on the B.C. coast, including the transport of logs in Clayoquot Sound in the 1950s and 1960s. He saw the need for change and believed passionately in decolonization of First Nations lands. Our kind friend, Chief Christopher Paul (1894-1976) of the Tsartlip people, was a traditional guardian of their lands. He was a crucial bridge between traditional land stewardship and present-day activism.

### Notes

1. Gordon Brent Ingram and Associates, 1230 Hamilton Street #204, Vancouver, B.C., V6B 2S8 — fax: (604) 669-2765.

2. See the book by Friends of Clayoquot Sound and Western Canada Wilderness Committee, *Meares Island: Protecting a Natural Paradise*, Western Canada Wilderness Society, Vancouver, 1985. For more information on the activities of the FOCS, see the "Time Line" in their Summer 1994 Handbook.

3. See the January 1991 report by the Clayoquot Sound Sustainable Development Task Force (B.C.), *Report to the Ministers of Environment and Regional and Economic Development*, Victoria, British Columbia, Ministry of Environment and Ministry of Regional and Economic Development.

4. There is a section in the 1993 film, "The Battle for the Trees," which discusses the loss of confidence by residents of Tofino in the Integrated Resource Management Process for Tofino Creek. An outline of this particular process is entitled "Clayoquot Sound Integrated Resource Management Planning Process for Tofino Creek," and is dated November 27, 1990. The report and related documents are on file with a number of provincial agencies in Port Alberni, British Columbia, in the Ministry of Forests and Ministry of Environment.

5. See the report by B. Austin, J. Hillaby, R. Laird, G. Porter, H. Quesnel, and G. Radcliffe (with G. Radcliffe editor), 1991. "Clayoquot Sound: Life support

services and natural diversity," Madrone Consultants Ltd., Victoria.

6. See Robert Prescott-Allen's "Clayoquot Sound Sustainable Development Strategy," *Forest Planning Canada* 8(1), 1991: 24-32.

7. See Valerie Langer's "Don't log the heart out of Clayoquot," *The Globe and Mail* (Toronto), May 3, 1993: A23.

8. See R. Matas' "Limited logging urged in B.C. rain forest," *The Globe and Mail* (Toronto), February 9, 1993: A1, A2.

9. See the final report of the "Clayoquot Sound Sustainable Development Strategy, Report to the Ministers of Economic Development, Small Business and Trade, Environment, Lands and Parks, and Forests by Robert Prescott-Allen, Strategy Director, and J. H. C. Walker, Chairperson, January 1993." In their January 14, 1993 cover letter, the authors of the report note, "we felt that continuing the process would provide diminishing returns with little hope of significant movement by the parties and termination of the process was the best option at this time."

10. There was some international involvement in Clayoquot before 1992, but with little coordination or the concept of a "campaign." One indicator of how the involvement of U.S. environmental groups intensified was the paid advertisement in the January 13, 1993 West Coast edition of *The New York Times* on page A9. The groups that were listed as supporting the statement were: Conservation International; Earth Island Institute; National Audubon Society; National Parks and Conservation Association; Rainforest Action Network; Sierra Club; The Wilderness Society; and the Western Ancient Forest Campaign.

11. See "The Government of British Columbia Response to the Commission on Resources and Environment's Public Report and Recommendations Regarding Issues Arising from the Clayoquot Land Use Decision," June 1, 1993, on file in the Office of the Premier, Victoria: page 2.

12. This report is on file with CORE in Victoria.

13. The government responses to the CORE recommendations were dated June 1, 1993, and are on file in the Office of the Premier, Victoria.

14. See News Release, "Government releases details of Clayoquot Sound forest practices." June 2, 1993, on file at the Ministry of Forests, Victoria.

15. See Elliot Diringer's two articles, "Canada's endangered rain forests— Ancient trees disappearing in 'Brazil of North'"; and "Northern woods: The other rain forest," *San Francisco Chronicle,* July 19, 1993: A1, A8 Col. 1.

16. This under-circulated report is on file at CORE in Victoria.

17. See D. Wilson's "Mass arrests in logging protest—RCMP round up more than 250 men, women and children in B.C.," *The Globe and Mail* (Toronto), August 10, 1993: A1 and A2; Deborah Wilson's "Taking a stand for the Sound," *The Globe and Mail,* August 14, 1993: A1 and A4; A. Gage, "Mahatma Gandhi and the forests of B.C.," *The Globe and Mail,* August 20, 1993: A17.

18. See Robert Sheppard, "Will B.C. sentence revive protesting?" *The Globe and Mail,* October 19, 1993: A25.

19. See *The Globe and Mail,* "Clayoquot protesters jailed 45 days for violating court order," October 15, 1993, page A1, and Clayton Ruby, "Following Gandhi in the rain forest," *The Globe and Mail,* October 26, 1993: A25.

20. *The Globe and Mail,* "Clayoquot protesters charged," October 20, 1993.

21. See *The Globe and Mail,* "B.C. government would welcome Liberal intervention in Clayoquot—Election promise offers Harcourt way out of logging issue," 25 October, 1993: A7.

22. For a discussion of the problems that might result from Federal intervention for preservation, see the discussions around South Moresby/*Gwaii Haanas* on the Queen Charlotte Islands. After a more protracted but perhaps less acrimonious struggle, and some smaller-scale blockades by the Haida Nation, there was a federal-provincial agreement for a national park reserve in 1988. But things have changed in five years. The South Moresby agreement has cost the Canadian taxpayer at least $109,000,000 and it is highly unlikely that such funds are available today. *Gwaii Haanas* involved one native group and two villages, while Clayoquot involves more communities and a number of bands and groups. Perhaps most problematic is that the rate of logging planned for the Clayoquot is a magnitude greater than what was occurring in the Queen Charlotte Islands five to ten years ago. If there was compensation given to the companies for loss of access to timber, the price to the Canadian taxpayer, in difficult economic times, would be too great for sufficient public support. For a chronology of the conservation efforts of the Haida, see G. B. Ingram, *in press.* "Institutional obstacles to conservation of habitat and biological diversity on *Gwaii Haanas,* British Columbia 1851-1993." *Forest and Conservation History* (North Carolina).

23. See the article in *The Globe and Mail,* "Clayoquot March," November 1, 1993: A4.

24. See Recommendation 1 of the Commission on Resources and Environment, page 8, *The Government of British Columbia Response to the Commission on Resources and Environment's Public Report and Recommendations Regarding Issues Arising from the Clayoquot Land Use Decision,* June 1, 1993, Victoria, Queen's Printer.

25. The Science Panel is Chaired by Professor Fred Bunnell of the University of British Columbia. The majority of the 19 members are employees of or consultants to the Government of British Columbia or dependent, to a large degree, on provincial research funds for their work. The recommendations of the Panel are due later in 1994. The group has released several important documents, including "Report of the Scientific Panel for Sustainable Forest Practices in Clayoquot Sound, January 31, 1994," which are on file with Cortex Consultants in Victoria.

26. See the "Canadian Press" article "B.C. slighted natives, report says," *The*

*Globe and Mail,* November 13, 1993: A3.

27. See *Proposed Forest Practices Rules for British Columbia,* Victoria, B.C. Ministry of Forests, November 1993.

28. The international campaign shifted to a boycott against B.C. timber and intensified in October of 1993. See Robert Mason Lee's "Worldwide campaign against logging hits forest firm," *The Vancouver Sun,* November 12, 1993: A1, A2. There was a committee of the European Parliament that visited Vancouver and Vancouver Island in January of 1994. For an example of the kinds of reports that went from B.C. to Europe, see Gordon Brent Ingram's "Report to the European Parliament—The Status of Biological Diversity and Ancient Forest Ecosystem in Clayoquot Sound, Vancouver Island, Canada," on file, Faculty of Forestry, The University of British Columbia.

29. See Charles Trueheart's "Tribes to share control of Vancouver Island rainforest (Hawiih Indian tribes assembly and government officials forged agreement defusing international protest against logging practices in Clayoquot Sound, Vancouver Island)," *Washington Post* v. 117, December 19, 1993: A34.

30. See Robert Sheppard's "Premier Harcourt's European vacation," *The Globe and Mail,* February 8, 1994: A19.

31. See Madeleine Drohan, "In Germany, Harcourt gets cutting advice," *The Globe and Mail,* February 3, 1994: B15; Keith Baldrey's "B.C. Indian leader slams Germans, Greenpeace," *The Vancouver Sun,* February 3, 1994: A1 and A2; and Brian Kennedy, "Harcourt conquered Greenpeace with help from aboriginal leader," *The Globe and Mail,* February 7, 1994: A3.

32. See Commission on Resources and Environment (CORE) (Province of British Columbia), *Vancouver Island Land Use Plan* Volume 1, February 1994, Victoria, CORE: 103-235.

33. See Patricia Lush, "Scott's British arm shuns firms cutting in Clayoquot," *The Globe and Mail,* March 1, 1994: B5.

34. At the signing ceremonies, only two environmental groups were recognized for their help and invited: Western Canada Wilderness Committee (WCWC) and the Natural Resources Defense Council (NRDC) through its association with Robert Kennedy Jr.

35. See Justine Hunter's "Keeping jobs deemed high priority for forestry chief," *The Vancouver Sun,* July 30, 1994: A3.

36. See "An independent environmental assessment of active and recent cutblocks in Clayoquot Sound and the Port Alberni Forest District," Greenpeace Clearcut Papers #3, July 1994. Prepared by Sierra Legal Defense Fund, Vancouver, for Greenpeace.

37. See Robert Mason Lee's "The pointed stick of Clayoquot has been dulled by repetition," *The Globe and Mail,* August 13, 1994: D2.

38. For some photographs of the logging methods under the label of "clearcut-

ting" that are typical in Clayoquot Sound, see pages 82 and 83, 86 and 87, 94 and 95 in *Clearcut: The Tragedy of Industrial Logging*, Bill Devall (editor), San Francisco, Sierra Club Books, 1993. Also the photos later in this volume.

39. See Tariq Banuri and Frédérique Apffel Marglin's 1993 "A systems-of-knowledge analysis of deforestation, participation, and management." In *Who Will Save the Forests? Knowledge, Power and Environmental Destruction*, T. Banuri and F. A. Marglin (editors), London, Zed Books: 1-23.

40. For a definition of "paradigm," those clusters of interrelated ideas so central to our worldviews, and a discussion of conflicts over scientific interpretation, see T. S. Kuhn, *The Structure of Scientific Revolutions* (Second Edition), Chicago, University of Chicago Press, 1970.

41. The concept of a "shift" or transition as opposed to a rupture in societal values—in the context of the structural economic crises of the raw resource extraction communities of B.C.—is optimistic to say the least. For a discussion of shifts in thinking, particularly the identification of full sets of alternatives in periods of decline in forest resources, see Banuri and Marglin's "The environmental crisis and the space for alternatives: India, Finland and Maine." In *Who Will Save the Forests? Knowledge, Power, and Environmental Destruction*: 24-52.

42. See Michael Valpy's discussion of civil disobedience in "Svend Robinson and the half-witted state," *The Globe and Mail*, July 27, 1994: A2.

43. For discussions of traditional communities of B.C. asserting their own perspectives for the conservation of natural ecosystems, see G. B. Ingram, 1990. "The need for knowledge from indigenous communities in planning networks of protected habitat for the conservation of biological diversity: Three island settings." In *Ethnobiology: Implications and Applications*. Proceedings of the First International Congress on Ethnobiology (Belem, Brazil, 1988). Part 2. M.J. Plotkin (ed.), Belem, Para, Goeldi Museum: 87-105.

44. I was not at the 1993 Peace Camp and Blockade myself. I stayed home and compiled background information. I had been involved in research on Clayoquot in the years before and was afraid, frankly, that the conflict would turn ugly. Three reports were completed for the Research Branch of the B.C. Ministry of Forests. They were authored by G. B. Ingram, W. K. Weiberg, N. A. Page and were entitled "Turning public concerns for the conservation of biological diversity and old-growth forest into operational criteria for land-use planning"; "The technical basis of landscape analysis for the conservation of biological diversity and old-growth attributes in the *CWH* Zone"; and "Generation of alternative sets of protected habitat, harvesting and silvicultural prescriptions for the conservation of biological diversity." These reports are on file at the Research Branch of the Ministry of Forests in Victoria.

45. There are two discussions of the Amazon Basin which are relevant in forming a definition of the process of underdevelopment for Clayoquot—whether or not the label "Brazil of the North" is justified. S. G. Bunker, *Underdeveloping the Amazon: Extraction, Unequal Exchange, and the Failure of the Modern State,*

Chicago, Illinois, University of Chicago Press, 1985; and S. Hecht and A. Cockburn, *The Fate of the Forest: Developers, Destroyers and Defenders of the Amazon*, New York, HarperCollins, 1990.

46. The only public documents showing the land-use decisions for Clayoquot Sound that were made by the Cabinet of British Columbia in April, 1993, were two small and vague documents authored by the Government of the Province of British Columbia, and entitled, *Clayoquot Sound Land Use Decision: Key Elements*, April 1993 (five pages including colour map); and *Clayoquot Sound Land Use Decision, Background Report*, April 1993, (15 pages including black and white map), Victoria, Queen's Printer for British Columbia.

47. See Joe H. Vogel and G. B. Ingram's 1993 "Biodiversity versus 'genetically coded functions': The importance of definitions in conservation policy," *RE-CIEL: Review of European Community & International Environmental Law* (London) 2(2): 121-125.

48. This part of Vancouver Island has probably been free of ice from the last glaciation for roughly 10,000 years. The type of forests that now dominate the area probably began to appear about 5,000 to 8,000 years ago.

49. For a discussion of the many ecological impacts and processes involved in the label "fragmentation," see G. B. Ingram, 1992. "Fragmentation: Towards an expanded model of the vulnerability of forest habitats on islands." Proceedings of the symposium, *In Harmony with Nature, International Conference on the Conservation of Tropical Biodiversity*. Kheong, Y. S. and L. S. Win (editors): 94-121. Kuala Lumpur, Malaysia, Malayan Nature Society.

50. G. B. Ingram, 1992. "The remaining islands with primary rainforest: A global resource," *Environmental Management* 16(5): 585-595.

51. For an initial definition of temperate "old-growth" forest, see Jerry F. Franklin's 1981 *Ecological Characteristics of Old-Growth Forest*, Portland, Oregon, United States Department of Agriculture Forest Service. For a review of the current research in the old-growth forests of B.C., see the various papers of the Old-Growth Strategy Task Force and its final report in 1992. Also see the related old-growth research paper on file in the Research Branch of the Ministry of Forests in Victoria. For a more current overview of the relationship of concerns for biological diversity, old-growth, and planning for both conservation and extractive development in the Pacific Northwest of the U.S., see D. S. Wilcover and J. T. Olson's "The ancient forests of the Pacific Northwest: A case study in conservation and economic development" In *Perspectives on Biodiversity: Case Studies of Genetic Resource Conservation and Development*, C. S. Potter, J. I. Cohen, and D. Janczewski (editors), Washington, D.C., American Association for the Advancement of Science: 177-185.

52. See G. Carleton Ray's 1988 "Ecological diversity in coastal zones and oceans." In *Biodiversity*, E. O. Wilson (editor), Washington, D.C., National Academy Press: 36-50.

53. For an example of a comprehensive approach to describing "deforestation"

and its social and economic dimensions, see David M. Kummer's 1993 *Deforestation in the Postwar Philippines,* Chicago and London: University of Chicago Press (University of Chicago Geography Research Paper. no. 234).

54. See G. P. Murdock's 1961 "Human influences on the ecosystems of high islands of the tropical Pacific." In *Man's Place in the Island Ecosystem,* a symposium, Tenth Pacific Science Congress, Honolulu, Hawai'i. F. R. Fosberg (editor). Honolulu, Hawai'i, Bishop Museum Press: 145-154.

55. For a look at the need for inventorying and monitoring in similar types of remote islands under pressure for logging, see G. B. Ingram's 1989 "Planning district networks of protected habitat for conservation of biological diversity: A manual with applications for marine islands with primary rainforest." Ph.D. dissertation in Environmental Planning. On file, University of California at Berkeley. Ann Arbor, Michigan, University Microfilms International.

56. For an outline of the principles of ecodevelopment, see J. L. McElroy and K. de Albuquerque's 1990 "Managing small-island sustainability: Toward a systems design." In *Sustainable Development and Environmental Management of Small Islands.* W. Beller, P. d'Ayala and P. Hein. Paris, Unesco/Parthenon: 43-55.

57. For an overview of the development of the concepts behind the international network of biosphere reserves, see Michel Batisse's 1982 "The biosphere reserve: a tool for environmental conservation and management," *Environmental Conservation* 9(2): 101-111; and Jane Robertson Vernhes' "Biosphere reserve: The beginnings, the present, and the future challenges." In *Proceedings of the Symposium on Biosphere Reserves.* Fourth World Wilderness Congress, 1989, Colorado, U.S.A. United States Department of the Interior, National Park Service, Atlanta, Georgia.

58. There was recently a network established for biosphere reserves on islands and for the establishment of additional areas. "Archipelago" is an information exchange network in the INSULA organization affiliated with Unesco. It can be contacted through Dr. Louis Brigand, Géosystemes, Université de Bretagne Occidentale, 6, avenue V. Le Gorgeu, 29275 Brest cedex, FRANCE — fax 33 98 31 66 26.

59. For a discussion of the links between the Share groups in B.C. and industry, see page 16 of Joyce Nelson's "Pulp and Propaganda," *The Canadian Forum* (July/August 1994): 14-19.

60. These are the names of the Ministries in 1993. Some of the names have since been changed.

61. For an indication of the slow rate of improvement in logging practices in B.C., see Gordon Hamilton's "Trees cut down under old rules in sensitive spots," *The Vancouver Sun,* July 21, 1994.

62. For a look at some of the issues emerging around the inventorying of biological diversity, see Paul R. Ehrlich and E. O. Wilson's "Prologue: Biodiversity Studies: Science and Policy." In *Perspectives on Biodiversity: Case Studies of Genetic*

*Resource Conservation and Development,* C. S. Potter, J. I. Cohen, D. Janczewski (editors), Washington, D.C., American Association for the Advancement of Science: ix-xiix.

63. The Convention was developed under the auspices of the United Nations Environment Programme, *Convention on Biological Diversity,* and is based on a June 1992 document on file in Nairobi at the Environmental Law and Institutions Programme Activity Centre. The Convention was ratified, with Canada as one of the original signatories, in December 1993.

64. See the report of James D. Darling and Kathleen E. Keogh of Tonguin Research Inc. of Tofino, entitled "Clayoquot Sound Biological Diversity Study Literature Review," in July 1990 (on file in Tofino) and the other report commissioned by Robert Prescott-Allen and authored by B. Austin, J. Hillaby, R. Laird, G. Porter, H. Quesnel, and G. Radcliffe (with G. Radcliffe editor), "Clayoquot Sound: Life support services and natural diversity," 1991.

65. See Robert Prescott-Allen's "Clayoquot Sound Sustainable Development Strategy," *Forest Planning Canada* 8(1), 1991: 24-32. For more comprehensive strategies for conservation which allow for development, see Michael E. Soulé's "Conservation: Tactics for a constant crisis" and Terry L. Erwin's "An evolutionary basis for conservation strategies." In P*erspectives on Biodiversity: Case Studies of Genetic Resources Conservation and Development,* C. S. Potter, J. I. Cohen, and D. Janczewski (editors), Washington, D.C., American Association for the Advancement of Science: 3-18 and 19-24 respectively.

66. See the criteria proposed by the Clayoquot Sound Sustainable Development Task Force (B.C.), in the *Report to the Ministers of Environment and Regional and Economic Development,* January 31, 1991, on file, British Columbia Ministry of Environment and Ministry of Regional and Economic Development, Victoria.

67. The best outlines of the "context" of the pressures for logging and conservation on Vancouver Island, as it applies to understanding how few "intact" watersheds remain, is Keith Moore's *An Inventory of Watersheds in the Coast Temperate Forests of British Columbia,* Earthlife Canada Foundation and Ecotrust/Conservation International, Vancouver, 1991. Clayoquot Sound has some of the most strategic wilderness watersheds remaining on Vancouver Island. Two different interpretations of satellite imagery are available that describe the situation: the "Vancouver Island Mosaic," produced in 1990 by the B.C. Ministry of Forests, Inventory Branch, Remote Sensing Section and a 1990 map published by the Sierra Club of Western Canada called "Our Vanishing Rainforest—Vancouver Island."

68. Prescott-Allen's final recommendations were in a report entitled "Clayoquot Sound Sustainable Development Strategy, Report to the Ministers of Economic Development, Small Business and Trade; Environment, Lands and Parks; and Forests—January 1993" [By Robert Prescott-Allen (Strategy Director) and J. H. C. Walker (Chairperson): 19 pp. + 5 appendices, (on file, Victoria, Government of British Columbia)]. As part of that report, there were a small number of areas, with very low timber values, where there was relative consen-

sus on establishment of protected areas. A blending of these "options" (pages 17-19) became the basis for the delineation of the April 1993 decisions. In the question period at the conference, "Conflict in the Clayoquot: A comprehensive analysis" (University of British Columbia, Vancouver, January 29, 1994), Mr. Mike Fenger, Forestry Specialist, Ministry of Environment, Lands and Parks, Government of British Columbia stated publicly that

1. the April 1993 decision was based nearly totally on the Prescott-Allan January 1993 recommendations, and
2. the recommendations were made under severe time constraints using only the current information available from the provincial government.

69. On the original government publication, this zone is coloured green, suggesting that it was actually going to be conserved. If present trends continue, these areas will probably involve standard and modified clearcut harvesting of ancient forest.

70. For an overview of the Scenic Corridors, see D. Bruce Whyte, David Minty, and Robert F. Gowan's "Visible areas analysis and classified satellite image analysis in support of scenic corridor management for Clayoquot Sound." Presented at GIS '94, Vancouver, February, 1994, Proceedings *in press*. Portions of the Scenic Corridor areas have already been logged over the last 50 years. The author's father was involved in these operations in the 1950s and '60s. The fact that more logging will take place in the Scenic Corridors means that the effective portion of the Clayoquot Sound planning area where liquidation of ancient forest can continue, albeit somewhat modified in some cases, is 59.9% of its total area. However, it must be remembered that this particular 59.9% of the Clayoquot Sound planning area contains the majority of remaining ancient forest ecosystems and habitat attributes.

71. The "new protected areas," delineated in the April 1993 decision, have been removed from consideration for timber harvesting and other industrial activities, although few of these areas currently have marketable timber and old-growth forest with high levels of biomass accumulation. Much of the "old-growth" conserved in these new protected areas consists of stunted shore forest with very small trees.

72. See G. B. Ingram's "Trade-off analysis in planning networks of protected areas for conservation of biological diversity," (accepted) *Biological Conservation.*

73. The best analysis of the types of habitat that are conserved in the protected areas created in the April 1993 Cabinet decision can be found in the 1993 *Ancient Rainforest at Risk: Final report of the Vancouver Island Mapping Project* of the Sierra Club of Western Canada, Victoria.

74. The categories of the Special Management Areas include: 3,000 hectares for Recreation (1.1% of the total of the Clayoquot planning area); 3,500 hectares for Wildlife (1.3%); and 40,000 hectares in Scenic Corridors (5.6%). Consequently, only 8% of the total of the Special Management Areas will have the conservation of biological diversity as its priority. This brings the total percentage of lands managed for maintenance of old-growth forest attributes and

processes as the primary concern to barely 34% of the total area of Clayoquot. What compounds the problem is that this particular 34% of Clayoquot Sound involves only a small portion of old-growth forest with big trees, high levels of biomass accumulation, and structural complexity.

75. At the time of the writing of this book, in August 1994, it is unclear how much timber was taken out of Clayoquot Sound in 1993. It is safe to say, however, that the corporations are taking as much old-growth timber as quickly as possible. This removal has not slowed in the Integrated Management Areas that were established in April 1993. The rate of cutting in the Scenic Corridors has barely slowed, if at all.

76. For two very different interpretations of new approaches to timber harvesting in the area, see Doug Hopwood's *Principles and Practices of New Forestry: A guide for British Columbians*, British Columbia Ministry of Forests, Victoria, 1991 and "An Alternative Silviculture and Harvesting Model for Upper Tofino Creek," by G. Natmiessnig and J. Weber and dated 1991 (on file Gundrich Natmessnig, A-9543 Arriach 40, Carinthia, Austria).

77. See Commission on Resources and Environment (CORE) (Province of British Columbia), *Vancouver Island Land Use Plan* Volume 1, February 1994, Victoria, CORE: 103-235.

78. See Herb Hammond, "Wholistic forest use: An ecosystem-based approach to timber management." In *Clearcut: The Tragedy of Industrial Forestry*, Bill Devall (editor), San Francisco, Sierra Club Books/Earth Island Press: 270-275.

79. See pages 21 and 22 in *The Government of British Columbia Response to the Commission on Resources and Environment's Public Report and Recommendations Regarding Issues Arising from the Clayoquot Land Use Decision*, June 1, 1993.

80. See page 23 in *The Government of British Columbia Response to the Commission on Resources and Environment's Public Report and Recommendations Regarding Issues Arising from the Clayoquot Land Use Decision*, June 1, 1993.

81. For an indication of the status of logging operations at the time of the printing of this article, see Glenn Bohn's "Greenpeace accuses MB of violations in Clayoquot," *The Vancouver Sun*, July 20, 1994: B3.

82. See V. Giacomini and V. Romani's 1978 "National parks as open systems: An Italian overview," *Landscape Planning* 5: 89-108.

83. See R. M. Pyle's 1980 "Management of nature reserves." In *Conservation Biology: An Evolutionary Perspective*, M. E. Soulé & B. A. Wilcox (editors), Sunderland, Massachusetts, Sinauer Associates: 319-328.

84. The first major outline of landscape ecology was R.T.T. Forman and M. Godron's *Landscape Ecology*, 1986, Toronto, John Wiley and Sons. There have been numerous articles and compilations subsequently that have great relevance to questions of reserve and cutblock size, shape, configuration, and connectivity.

85. For a discussion of indicators for monitoring the status of local biological diversity on the B.C. coast, see G. B. Ingram's 1992 "Landscape indicators for conservation of biological diversity: An example from Haida Gwaii, British Columbia." In *Landscape Approaches to Wildlife and Ecosystem Management.* G. B. Ingram and M. R. Moss (editors). Morin Heights, Quebec, Polyscience: 99-134.

86. C. S. Holling (editor), *Adaptive Environmental Assessment and Management.* John Wiley, Chichester, New York, 1978.

87. See Reed Noss, and L. D. Harris' 1986 "Nodes, networks, and MUMs: Preserving diversity at all scales," *Environmental Management* 10 (3): 299-309.

88. See R. F. Noss' 1990 "Indicators for monitoring biodiversity: A hierarchical approach," *Conservation Biology* 4(4): 355-364; and G. B. Ingram's 1992 "Fragmentation: Towards an expanded model of the vulnerability of forest habitats on islands." Proceedings of the symposium, *In Harmony with Nature, International Conference on the Conservation of Tropical Biodiversity.* Kheong, Y. S. and L. S. Win (editors): 94-121. Kuala Lumpur, Malaysia, Malayan Nature Society.

89. For a relevant example of integrating the conservation of habitat and visual resources through principles of landscape ecology, see N. Diaz and D. Apostol's *Forest Landscape Analysis and Design: A Process for Developing and Implementing Land Management Objectives for Landscape Patterns,* U.S. Department of Agriculture Forest Service, Gresham, Oregon.

90. Two of the most relevant discussions of "gap analysis" are F. W. Burley's 1988 "Monitoring biological diversity for setting priorities in conservation," in *Biodiversity,* E. O. Wilson (editor), Washington, D.C., National Academy Press: 227-230; and the monograph for J. M. Scott, F. Davis, B. Csuti, R. Noss, B. Butterfield, C. Groves, H. Anderson, S. Caicco, F. D'Erchia, T. C. Edwards, J. Ulliman, and R. G. Wright—the 1993 "Gap Analysis: A geographic approach to protection of biological diversity," Supplement to the *Journal of Wildlife Management* 57(1), *Wildl. Monog.* 123: 1-41.

91. G. B. Ingram and J. T. Williams' 1993 "Gap analysis for in situ conservation of crop genepools: Implications of the Convention on Biological Diversity." *Biodiversity Letters* (London) 1: 141-148.

92. In the last year, very little of the regular operating budgets of the provincial and federal Canadian agencies has gone to inventories of the Clayoquot area or to evaluations of the April 1993 decision. There is a fund for research under the Canada and British Columbia Forest Resource Development Agreement II (FRDA), but these funds have been limited to implementation of the April 1993 decision, with few additional inventories. None of these funds has been applied to independent scientific review of the long-term impacts of the April 1993 decision.

93. See the June 2, 1993, Province of British Columbia News Release, Ministry of Forests and Ministry of Environment, Lands and Parks, entitled "Government releases details of Clayoquot Sound Forest Practices." The high-

lights of the changes include: "adding four new staff on the ground in Clayoquot to make sure all logging operations in environmentally-sensitive areas are monitored at least once a week"; "an end to large-scale clearcuts, replaced with small, dispersed cut blocks averaging 10 to 40 hectares"; "reducing road building"; "protection of biodiversity values"; and "increased use of harvesting alternatives, such as helicopter and skyline logging, particularly in sensitive areas."

94. See the Government of British Columbia's November 1993, *British Columbia Forest Practices Code, Rules and Discussion Paper,* Victoria, Queen's Printer.

95. This report is on file with Cortex Consultants, Victoria.

96. Unfortunately, "watersheds" can also be used as a codeword for "get the islands," since the islands in Clayoquot Sound have some of the best timber, and they can be whittled away one-by-one without concern for maintenance of their ecosystems. Islands like Flores and Vargas should be recognized as having value for protection of their integrity. Conflicts over logging in Clayoquot increasingly will be over a multitude of smaller watersheds, with each conflict, singly, not being very spectacular.

97. Two discussions of the difficulties of "integrating" visual resources into land-use decision-making are D. Wood's 1988 "Unnatural illusions: Some words abut visual resource management," *Landscape Journal* 7(2): 192-206; and G. B. Ingram's 1991 "Habitat, visual and recreational values and the planning of extractive development and protected areas: a tale of three islands," *Landscape and Urban Planning* 21: 109-129.

98. See the "Key questions and answers" page in the March 19, 1994 Province of B.C. News Release, "Interim Measures Agreement on Clayoquot Sound signed by the Central Region Chiefs of the Nuu-chah-nulth Tribal Council and the Province."

99. On page 15 of *Progress Report 2,* the Scientific Panel highlights the traditional system of land and resource management called *HaHuulhi.*

100. See page 218 in G. B. Ingram's "Rainforest conservation initiated by traditional island communities: Implications for development planning," *Canadian Journal of Development Studies* (Ottawa) XV(2): 193-218; and page 45 of Paul Virilio's *Popular Defense & Ecological Struggles,* New York, Semiotext[e], 1990 (1978), translated by Mark Polizzoitti.

The author wishes to thank Ron and Veronica Hatch and a number of members of Friends of Clayoquot Sound, particularly Garth Lenz and Valerie Langer, for their contributions.

# The Clayoquot Papers

DR. MAURICE GIBBONS

These pieces about the protest at Clayoquot Sound and the struggle to stop the mismanagement and misuse of our forests began as items in my journal written during the unfolding events of my involvement, arrest and trial. I am proud to be a part of that protest, but the honour for its successful impact on logging policies and practices in British Columbia must go to the young people who organized it, managed it and manned the front lines for months in relative anonymity and at considerable risk to themselves and their futures. Their dedication, sacrifice, vision and competence assures me that there is a new generation coming that may yet save the planet from our plundering.

## On the Line at Clayoquot

On August the 9th, 1994, my wife, Margot, and I were arrested at the Kennedy River Bridge in Clayoquot Sound for refusing to obey a court injunction against obstructing the logging operations of MacMillan Bloedel employees in the area. We are not activists; we have never been arrested before; we were deeply shaken by the experience.

People ask, "Why did you do it?" Our answer is that we believe that the forests and other resources of B.C. belong to all of us, and that we have both a right and a responsibility to speak and act when we think they are being misused. We think that falling any more of the old-growth rainforests on Vancouver Island is misuse, especially if the timber is clearcut and then shipped abroad as whole logs rather than as products we make from them. We feel that we need to take action for ourselves, for our grandchildren and for their children. We want them to know that we did not sit idly by while their treasure, their inheritance that we hold in trust, was destroyed. When the government announced that two-thirds of Clayoquot Sound would be logged, our journey to Kennedy River Bridge began.

We phoned the Sound Majority in Victoria offering to help, and on Saturday, August 7th, we received a call back from Friends of Clayoquot Sound asking us to be at The Bridge on Monday for a special rally. We packed up, caught an early Sunday ferry to Nanaimo and drove to the Peace Camp, a scattering of tents and tarps perfectly situated in "The Black Hole," a mountainside sheared to stumps and burned to embers. A vegetarian dinner for 300 residents was underway. The young leaders were organizing a circle meeting to discuss strategy and training sessions in civil disobedience for newcomers. As an educator, I was impressed by the participation of the children and youths in the camp, and the respect shown for their contributions.

That night we stayed at Tur na nog, a bed and breakfast in Tofino run by Sile Simpson, who it turns out, had been arrested three times in Clayoquot and was currently confined to her house rather than a cell only because of her children. We talked into the night with a drop-in group of Sile's friends and had to be prodded out of bed at 3:30 a.m. to drive back to the camp. We arrived just in time to join a cavalcade of cars, trucks and buses carrying over 1,000 people as it turned off the highway onto a dusty logging road heading for the Bridge. After several kilometers, marshals told us to pull over, park and walk. As the crowd gathered in the breaking dawn, the drums and singing began. Nothing had really happened yet, but I felt my heart thumping.

The crowd assembled as a noisy mob until someone held up a hand. Soon there was a forest of hands and suddenly, complete silence. This was the first sign of discipline, order and strategy that characterized the protesters throughout this amazing day. Signs and speeches reminded us all that this was a peaceful, orderly, drug-and-alcohol-free protest. With feelings running high and talk of blowing the bridge among the most passionate, control was a challenging task. One of our three guides, Tzeporah Berman, stood on top of a van with a microphone, welcomed us, and set the scene. "If the loggers are coming, they will be here between 5:45 and 6:00. You have until then to decide if you will be arrested today. If this is the day, simply stay on the road." Margot turned to me and said, "If we are going to make a stand, it has to be today. With so many people, this is the day that will count." I agreed and we walked onto the road.

As people waited, a chant started behind us, "If we all stay on the road, they can't arrest us all!" and soon everyone was chanting to the beat of the drums. Then we were instructed to sit. People with arm ribbons came to take our names and addresses. Others followed to write the phone numbers of lawyers on the palms of our hands. We were urged to get buddies who would look after our cars and track us through the arrest process from outside the jail. I found Sam Meisle who did all of those things for us and almost immediately brought us sandwiches, "For jail." Others came by and asked, "Are you all right?" or "Do you need anything?" Several stopped to touch us or hug us and say, "We're so glad to have you here." Suddenly in the hubbub a hand went up and in seconds a thousand people were silent again.

Margot whispered to me, "It's nearly 7:30. They're not coming." William Thomas, told us on the PA, "We respect all beings and we do not engage in violence, no matter how badly we are provoked. The company man will read the injunction and ask us to disperse. Then the RCMP will announce that you will be arrested if you don't move, and finally, they will carry or walk you to the buses. If you feel threatened at any time, hold up one finger and one of us will be there immediately."

Then the helicopters from TV stations arrived and circled the blockade, giving the scene an Apocalypse Now atmosphere. Teams of newspaper, radio and TV people appeared everywhere, shooting and interviewing. One American TV announcer stood beside us and spoke into his camera, "In this summer of discontent, dozens of people have been arrested...." Cries of protest interrupted him. "Not dozens—hundreds!" He stalked off, snarling, "Screw these jerks." We never saw him again. Someone had just yelled, "It's nine o'clock and no trees are falling in Clayoquot Sound!" when Valerie Langer announced, "We have just learned that the loggers are on their way." A cheer went up. They had chosen to give us this confrontation. We never figured out why, unless they hoped—as the rumour went—to show us up as an unruly mob. The protest would have fizzled without them; and when the crummies finally went through, there were no loggers in them. The company was not even trying to get its men to their workplace.

We began reaching out to each other and introducing ourselves—a secretary, two teachers, another professor, a corporate accountant, a nurse, a mother with two kids, a grad-school student, a mechanic, a pediatrician. Our conversation stopped in mid-sentence as a MacMillan Bloedel pick-up truck rolled into sight with a scowling man standing like Patton behind the cab. Police cars, buses and huge logging trucks with their piggy-backed bunks pulled up to the blockade perimeter and loomed behind him. While he read the court injunction against our protest, another employee walked among us with a video camera, scowling and holding the lens up to our faces as if to say, "We've got you now!" People began leaving the road for the perimeter as the RCMP announced that we would be placed under arrest if we did not move. For a moment it seemed that only a few of us would be left, but when the dust settled, more than 300 people remained on the road.

A logger made a speech, asking us to let him go to work. A

handful of loggers' wives walked up the road among us, wearing the yellow ribbons of Share, their support organization. They joked and laughed nervously, not knowing quite what to do. Neither did we. Our struggle was with MacMillan Bloedel and the NDP, not them; our opposition is to clearcutting the last of our irreplaceable old-growth, not to logging.

The RCMP began arresting people and carrying them to the buses. You could walk or go limply passive and be carried. A chant started up and grew to thunder, "The whole world is watching... Shame!" In the cacophony of helicopters, drums, chanting, cameras and urgent loudspeaker announcements about our rights, the tension grew. Margot and I tightened our grip on each other. The police came closer and closer. In front of us, they tried to grab a young, mentally handicapped boy from his mother and he began screaming. Other children, calm up to this point, began to cry. Support people closed in followed by cameras. Margot said, "I won't go if we can't go together." Three officers came to us. I said, "Help us both up and we'll walk," and they did. As we left, I turned and called out, "It was an honour to be here with you on this day," and I meant it.

There were so many of us that the recreation hall in Ucluelet had to be pressed into service as a jail. When we walked in at about 10:00 a.m. the first bus-load stood and cheered, as we all did for the next bus and the bus after that. When everyone was assembled we held hands in a circle around other circles, sang our songs and ended, with very 60's warmth, in a mass hug. The RCMP charged us, photographed us and required us to sign guarantees that we would not block the road again. Around 6:30 P.M. we were released until our court date in Victoria on August 12th. Although swamped by the largest protest arrest in Canadian history, the police remained courteous and professional. As someone said about this very civil disobedience, "Only in Canada." When we left, Sam was waiting with our car. That night the Clayoquot protest was the lead story across the country without a window being broken or a shot fired.

# The Journey: Encounters with Trees

My journey to Clayoquot began long before the summer of 1993. Trees—the forests, the wilderness—were an important part of my life and a shaping influence upon me from my earliest years. The same must be true for most British Columbians. When the call came to protest our disappearing old-growth rainforests, it seemed natural, almost required, for me to go. These episodes in my story tell why.

* * *

As a child I seemed always to be in the trees. They were my refuge and playground. We climbed high up vine maples to kick out and ride the tops down again. Fresh from a Johnny Weismuller Tarzan movie, we took turns sitting in the big tree holding a swing-rope, gathering the courage to launch out into that long dizzying swoop to our wind-shattered tree fort in the branches opposite. We watched in awe as our classmates, Albert and Pee Wee, climbed to the tops of tall cedar trees, dropped their home-made bombs, blew out foot-square chunks of pavement, and when the sirens wailed, slid down spread-eagled on the outside of the branches with amazing speed and scurried into the woods. I would sit for hours unseen as high up as I could climb into the raftered green of the huge maple tree in our backyard, sitting quietly, feeling the wind moving in the branches I clung to, commanding my cutter in full sail around the Horn in pursuit of wily buccaneers; or watching the real war games unfolding before me on English Bay. The trees held me as often as anyone in my family ever did.

Vancouver was a city on the edge of wildness. You could walk up any street on the North Shore, pass the last house and step onto a trail into wilderness that could wind all the way to the Arctic Circle. I grew up on that edge, moving easily from the city to the woods and back. Like living in trees, living among them was a powerful experience. Whenever a crisis arose, I turned instinctively to a quiet place in the forest. If the family centre wouldn't hold, if professional opponents conspired to do me in, if someone I loved was dying, I went to where the pavement ends and passed into the reflective solitude of a wilderness grove to think the problem through. In that great calm I could hear my voice, encounter my feelings and find a pathway forward. The night my brother was shot down in Europe I walked into the woods. As dawn broke in the clearing where I sat, sunlight fell on a moss covered nurse-log thick with the seedlings and saplings of new growth. "Cedar tree falling among shoots," I wrote of my first metaphysical thought; even in death there is life. With this understanding, in this eternal place, my healing began.

In the woods I feel a presence I cannot define, a "force that through the green fuse drives the flower," an aesthetic intelligence organizing this profusion of life in perfect disarray, a power much greater than mine, than ours, flowing through this ever unfolding landscape with only one imperative—to create life. When I go to one of my wild places and become quiet, reflective, it is this presence that I feel, and a primal connection with it. All gods were born in such places. Our metaphors are rooted in, and arise from, nature. Surely, sanity is a wild place where we renew ourselves, our nature; and madness is an urban place of concrete and straight lines, where we see only ourselves looking back at us everywhere, masters of a lifeless universe. We need a world with two hemispheres as certainly as our brains do: one wild and natural, the other ordered and structured. Our hope is the holographic merging of wild and ordered minds in people determined to ensure both a wild and ordered future.

Few wild places create a greater sense of awe than groves of the huge ancient trees in the temperate rainforests of Vancouver Island, such as those in Clayoquot Sound. In these sacred places, the grandest trees are as much as fifteen hundred years old and spiral up as high as three hundred feet. Such forests—standing long before Captains Cook or Vancouver, long before Columbus, before the crusades, even before Charlemagne—are our ancient monuments, our cathedrals: the oldest, largest living things in our land. Once taken down, they are gone forever. What little is left is disappearing fast. Will we defend and preserve our old-growth rainforests for their spiritual, aesthetic and recreational values, as well as their environmental necessity and great commercial value, or will we once again find ourselves saying, "Gone! How did we ever let that happen?"

* * *

My childhood solitudes were shattered in my fifteenth summer when I found myself on the way to a remote logging camp in Holberg Inlet on the northwest coast of Vancouver Island, hired on as a whistle punk, a kind of signalman. Logging gave the boy a chance to become a man, taught me how to work and over the span of six years put me through school and university.

The first morning at Holberg float camp, when 450 men assembled on the wharf, everyone was mustered into a crew except me; I was forced on one crew boss—"Charlie, you take this kid!"—by his boss. For ten days no one at that site said anything to me, a lethal summer wonder, except the barest descriptions of my job, and I didn't know what to do about it. I had never seen anything so dramatic as our workplace. From the hillside we were logging we looked straight down a valley crowded with trees as far as we could see. On the hillside across from us you could hear fallers yell and watch the slow swish of those huge trees to the ground. Nearby, a highrigger was climbing a huge fir tree, trimming the branches as he went, topping it to be our next spar tree, then sitting on the top, 120 feet up, to have lunch and talk to the men below. Some logs we pulled into the pile swayed and surged forward like battering rams, ploughing and smashing everything ahead of them. Some were ten feet or more thick; the biggest enough to be a truckload by themselves.

It took twelve work days to earn enough to go home, and I couldn't wait to leave. On the twelfth day we were setting up at the new spar tree. The enormous mainline and haulback blocks were hung but needed to be threaded with pencil-thin strawline that would haul the heavy yarding cables through them and out for several hundred yards in a wide clothesline loop back to the yarding machine. Chokers hung from a steel plate that was pulled out to the bush by the haulback, and pulled back by the mainline, dragging logs into a pile around the spar tree. The hooker asked, "Who's goin' up to thread the f____ing blocks?" Everyone kept silent until I heard myself say, "I will." They sat me in a loop of chain on a thin line, handed me the strawline I was to thread through the blocks, and suddenly I was hurtling up the tree. Strawline is light to lift, but holding a hundred feet of it can tax even a strong person. I quickly spun the loose end around the line that was carrying me and clamped it with my hands, but as I did so I raced past the blocks toward the top of the tree. I tried to yell but no noise came out. I waved, but no one was looking up. I saw myself flying off into space, but two feet from the small block at the top of the tree, they stopped and then slowly lowered me in bumps to the big blocks. I put the loose end of the strawline I was carrying through the mainline block, hooked it onto my chain seat and then let go of the slack I was holding. As they lowered me down, the straw line was pulled through the blocks.

When I landed, no one said a word, but something was different. Perhaps I was supposed to be scared but not successful. We worked hard that day hauling out lines, getting ready to log, and when I walked toward the crummy at quitting time, I was so tired I didn't think I could scramble over the tailgate into a seat. Suddenly the hooker melted out of the woods beside me and, lifting me up by the back of my pants said, loud enough for the others to hear, "You're going to be okay, kid." They were the sweetest words I ever heard, and as vivid in my mind now as they were then. The twelve-day deadline completely forgotten, I worked all summer with the fifteen men on our crew. I was proud to be one of them, to feel that I knew how to do a man's work and to know that I had earned my pay. But I cannot forget the image of that once lush valley as we topped the hill on my last trip to camp before going home: as far as the eye could see, there was not a tree left standing.

\* \* \*

No other experience better prepared me for environmental radicalization than what happened to our summer camp on Porpoise Bay, the body of water that makes a peninsula of the land from Sechelt to Earl's Cove on the Sunshine Coast. As a struggling young husband and father, I was delighted to find that the forestry branch would occasionally, for a small fee, issue special use permits for plots of land in some of its reserves. A forester gave us a tour of the plots available and we selected one on a beautiful little bay in the wilds about eight miles up Porpoise Bay from Tillicum Fish Camp. For each of the next five summers my wife, two children and I paddled our canoe to this treasured retreat and set up camp.

The sand and pebbles of our beach stretched about two hundred yards between two arms of rock that came together another two hundred yards behind the beach making a delta-like triangle of land divided by a small stream that emptied into the bay. We cleared a camp space beside the stream in the thick cover of cedars, fir, hemlock, yew and alder. From our driftwood table we looked up Salmon Inlet to the peaks of the Tantalus mountains. The forest and ocean teemed with birds and animals. At night we often swam wrapped in the purple glow of the phosphorescent waters, then lay by the fire looking up at a sky crowded with stars and went to sleep waiting for the next meteorite to streak across the heavens. It remains a special place for all of us, and at its heart was the magical stream pouring from its cool mossy canyon and winding among the trees. If camp became a spiritual experience, our creek was at the heart of it. Years later I described it as,

> A perfect disorder of waters
> Spilling over stones;
> Pure spirit moving in music
> Under cedar boughs
> To the waiting sea.

At the end of our fifth season we stopped in to discuss our permit fee for the next year with the forester. He warned us that loggers would be taking out a dozen trees about a quarter of a mile up the creekbed on our property. I stopped the logger foreman on the road and was assured that the logs would be removed with minimum damage to the site. The next year we made our first trip early to clear a space for the cabin we planned to build. As we paddled around the first arm of rock, and camp came into view, we stopped in grim and silent disbelief. Every tree on either side of our lot and right to the beach was gone; only stumps remained. A derelict yarding machine the size of a bus was dug in across the stream bed and surrounded by rusting cables. The logs coming down the canyon and across the landing had ploughed out everything to the raw rock and deposited it in a wall of broken tree trunks, boulders and other debris fifty feet deep about a hundred feet back from shore. The stream, now diverted, fanned out across the property removing a wide swath of soil and depositing tons of rock and gravel from upstream. Camp as we knew it was gone and in its place an ugly, devastated war-zone. My wife and daughter cried. My daughter remembers it as one of the worst traumas and shaping experiences of her youth.

I tried to continue with our cabin plans. Late one afternoon, while I was cutting and burning, I heard a motor coming into the bay. The logger, holding his launch off the rocks with a pike pole, called out, "Sorry about the mess. My fallers got a bit out of control." He was taking his men home from work and I could see their faces laughing at me through the portholes as I stood amongst that wreckage with a double-bitted axe in my hands, furious and helpless. We complained to the forester. The logger, we were told later, was fined $50.00 per stump, but allowed to keep the logs. This experience became my metaphor for logging and the land. The industry has never given me a reason to change it. Last week a logger said into TV cameras, "If there is one tree left and it will put food on the table for my wife and kids, I'll cut it down." I wonder if a fisherman said the same thing about the last fish the year before they shut down our totally decimated eastern fishery? We never went back to Porpoise Bay.

* * *

In 1969, during my first class as a university professor, my students began my education in environmental issues. With a brand new doctorate in hand and filled to the very top with knowledge, I began the lecture reading from my erudite notes. They gave me a half-hour's grace and then someone said, "Maurice, what the hell are you talking about?" I put my notes aside and we began a conversation that continued through most of the course. As one young woman said, "It's hard to get excited about philosophies of education when the threat of nuclear war has convinced many of us that we likely won't live to be thirty."

I focused quickly on the first key question in my course, "What is the most important thing to teach?" The issues that they raised surprised me. In the two decades that separated us the world and our youth had changed dramatically. Among more familiar topics, they listed such items as, nuclear holocaust, the establishment and power, global conflicts, space, technology, information and the new media and race and gender equality. But the key issue for them was the environment.

"We are destroying our planet," they said, "and we have to do something about it." As a start, we listed all the environmental crises we could think of and soon filled every blackboard in the classroom with such items as pollution, extinct and endangered species, resource depletion, desertification, deforestation, overpopulation, urbanization, starvation and disease. The list seemed endless. What astounded the students most was that they could not find any reference to these issues in the official school curriculum or assigned textbooks. Students could spend twelve years in school and never address the state of their own planet. I was caught in no-man's-land, too. I had followed Rachel Carson's heroic battle with pesticide companies and their scientists over _Silent Spring_, but I was basically uneducated about the environment and began scrambling to catch up.

We came next to the second question, "What is the best way to teach the topic you choose?" After lengthy discussion we decided that experience was more important than information and drama was more important than drill. Someone noticed that many students in the class had special performance skills, another suggested, "Let's do a production," and everyone agreed. They named their one hour call-to-action "Earthrise" after the image of the planet, seen from the Apollo spacecraft, rising blue and glowing from behind a desolate grey moonscape. Using film and slides, the students contrasted that stunning view of earth with the uglier close-up realities of pollution, population and environmental disaster. Two dancers began in love and joy, but that turned to anguish at the sights they saw, and ended in robotic, automated isolation. After a series of brief vignettes of human indifference to planetary degradation, the actors faced a decision between taking action or facing an atomic explosion that filled all the screens in the room. "Earthrise or earthfall?" they asked; "It depends on you."

Working with these students was an education; they taught me well. Five years later, asking myself the first curriculum question, I decided that the most important things to teach next were their environmental ideals. In partnership with an elementary school principal and friend, the late Andy Neuman, I launched World Citizens for a Global Generation, which promoted programmes designed to teach students to be responsible citizens of planet earth, loving members in the family of humankind, responsible stewards of the environment, practitioners of the peaceful resolution of conflict, and organizers determined to plan the future rather than let it happen by chance, for better or for worse. The main principle is that responsible citizens take informed action. Students choose their issues, study them from all sides and then decide what action they will take. Some of the Clayoquot participants could be graduates of a World Citizen's program. I would be very proud if some were. Democracies survive only as long as there are people determined to preserve them; natural environments endure only as long as there are people prepared to nurture and defend them.

\* \* \*

During a holiday with the family on Saltspring Island, when I was about forty years old, I stumbled upon a new career which changed my relationship to trees and timber completely. With a reputation as a kid who was "bright enough but no good with his hands," I was unprepared for what happened when I went to the beach to supervise my small children at play in the water, picked up a piece of driftwood, unclasped my pocketknife and absent-mindedly began to whittle. The cedar released a pungent perfume as I cut; the grain patterns changed as each shaving curled and fell away. Soon I noticed the shape of a woman's body emerging and began consciously to complete the vision that I saw. As an acknowledged klutz, I was surprised at the quality of what I had done, and when I set it up on the deck table, so were others.

Afterwards, I started reading books on carving and sculpture, purchased a few carving tools and then began collecting carvable woods. Many different people became my informal teachers over the years, including a pair of Makonde carvers in Dar es Salaam, Tanzania, a furniture carver in Chiang Mai, Thailand, a master carver in Mas, Bali, and a craftsman from Sydney, Australia. The ebony, which was so plentiful in East Africa when I was there in 1972, was logged out for fast profit; the teak of Thailand, once thought inexhaustible, has almost all been shipped abroad as logs; the many beautiful eucalyptus timbers I carved for an exhibition in Australia were rare then and only recently became regulated; and the Balinese are now reduced to carving woods they would have thought beneath them, perhaps unholy, to carve before. As the demand for wood increases, availability decreases, and the value skyrockets, placing even greater pressure on disappearing timber resources everywhere.

No wood sculptor in British Columbia can carve without being influenced by the work of West Coast Native artists, their spiritual relationship with trees and their peoples' history of utilization of all that the red cedar can provide. Like the carvers of totems and masks, I draw my imagery from nature, from the shapes of bark, snags, roots and rot. One of my early exhibitions was a series of kings, studies in power, all derived from forest images: one king was tormented by the roots of his own treachery, another rotted from corruption, a third was hollow as a burnt-out snag in his emptiness and a fourth was wise with forest light shining through him.

Carving, for me, is a meditation fed by journal sketches of observations and sculptural ideas. The mind struggles until a vision forms, and with it, the desire to see that vision made real. Then with the right wood and sharpened tools, the rough shaping begins. As the image appears, the vision shifts; the piece takes on a life of its own. Concentrating with greater and greater intensity, slipping deeper into total absorption, the cutter in my hand appearing to move on its own, I seem to become one with the wood, out of myself, beyond the shop, the house and even time. As native carvers were reported to do, I ask the spirit of the wood to let me in, to share its power with me. The next piece is never certain in art. I can only hope that the wood will.

Artists put themselves into the timber and try to shape the spirit of it as beautifully as possible. With such devotion to wood and such intensity of interaction with it, I am especially distressed that we still allow whole logs and cants—logs trimmed square to class them as lumber—to be shipped abroad unworked, and with them, the jobs and increased value that making products from them will provide. One of our oldest most beautiful woods, yellow cedar, is rare and only grows in the Pacific Northwest. This incredible close-grained ancient timber, which fills any workshop with its incense and comes up in carving like ivory, is so highly regarded by some countries it is sliced into the thinnest veneer and used to finish other products. We are, to those countries, their East Africa, their Thailand. It's one tragedy to lose such magnificent old-growth, a second tragedy to see it sold cheap, one-time only, for quick profit. And a third to see all the special industries, skilled jobs and long-term profits go with them. The spirits of such trees as our yellow cedars are mute; we must speak for them.

\* \* \*

Each of us brings a different history to the next event in our lives, and that history guides our decisions about what the next event will be. I want to believe that what we do next will save our rainforests. I want to believe, with Arthur Schopenhauer, that, "All truth passes through three stages. First, it is ridiculed. Second, it is violently opposed. Third, it is accepted as self-evident." The road to truth and preservation, however, often seems incredibly long and strewn with obstacles. When the struggle moves valley by valley, when we seem to slide back from each piece of ground we gain, I want to shout, "Wake up!" The form of writing that most resembles a shout is satire, but as one reader observed about the following piece, "These days it will likely be read as reporting."

## Let's Clear-Cut Stanley Park Now

Jonathan Slash
CEO, Lamprey Logging Co

Since the government has confirmed that it will clear-cut most of the old-growth temperate rainforest in Clayoquot Sound, and since a recent Angus Reid survey shows that a majority of British Columbians agree with that decision, the stage is set for us to harvest the prime timber close at hand in Vancouver's Stanley Park. We are shocked and dismayed to find that, because of misleading information, we cut far too many trees all these years and planted far too few. The fact is that we have to log the Park to save the industry. There will, no doubt, be the usual rabid resistance to this modest proposal, but we have every assurance that it will be dealt with as forcefully and efficiently as have other protests in this province recently.

If we log Stanley Park now, many desperately needed jobs will be created, and provincial revenues will be greatly increased. Serving our workers and the community is, of course, our company's prime imperative. As for operations, nearby Coal Harbour will provide a convenient deep-sea port for the direct export of unworked logs that has proved so profitable in Thailand and Costa Rica as well as British Columbia. But revenue would not come from log sales alone. Some of the timber could be value-added in a mill built on Deadman's Island, a sacred Indian burial ground that was clear-cut early in this century and is as good a mill-site now as it was then.

Logs and lumber would not be the only source of jobs and revenue in the park. We would set up a broadly representative committee to agree that once the land is cleared, 2.6% could possibly be replanted as sustainable forest for the spiritual enhancement of the community. The committee will then decide to develop the rest of the Park into the Manhattan of the West, one of the richest residential-commercial developments in North America and the jewel—the soul—of Vancouver, with jobs and profits for everyone. Think of the land sales, waterfront, construction, office towers, hotels, highways, sub-divisions, rentals and services. Simply staggering possibilities for those with the vision to build something of value where now there is only bush.

Why wait? Many of the big trees in the park have already blown down, others are getting old, many with only three or four hundred years of life left. It is only a matter of time before the whole remaining forest catches fire, and then we will all watch potential jobs and profits go up in smoke, lost forever. We must log now. No spotted owls or other rare species survive in the park; we will make sure of that. The forest we replant, a park-within-a-park, will be back just like it is now in less than a century, not the 1500 years it will take to regenerate the old-growth dinosaurs we are taking out of Clayoquot Sound. And of course our logging practices will be rigorously controlled by the forest service armed with new, much stiffer penalties than the lesser penalties they seldom, if ever, imposed on logging companies before. Now that the government is a major investor in the industry, people can rest assured that their officials will be especially rigorous in hunting down and prosecuting logging malpractice, no matter what the impact is on the value of company shares.

The technical studies by our department of corporate intelligence show that only 4.08% of visitors to the Park ever leave the perimeter and enter the forest itself. Cars pass through the Park carrying passengers between Vancouver and the North Shore about five million times annually. The main concern among these commuters is that logging would destroy the beauty they drive through every day. To solve this problem, we propose leaving "aesthetic forest fringes"—made popular at Clayoquot—to line both the highway and the ocean perimeters. Thus, the park experience will be virtually unchanged for 95.02% of visitors even after 97.4% of it has been clear-cut. Citizens can have their park and log it, too.

Professional, tree-hugging environmentalists—and the crowd of disheveled welfare hippie malcontents that follows them—will be predictably outraged with this proposal. But as events in Clayoquot Sound this summer have shown, these rag-tag agitators are no match for the collective power of the courts, the police, the Attorney General's office, the government and the most powerful corporation in the land. When democracy and corporate profits were threatened we all worked together to restore order swiftly and efficiently with stiff jail sentences, fines and criminal records. Take note protesters, especially you people on pensions and you unemployed mothers whose children should be in school learning something important, if such interference is repeated in the Park, our judges and legislators assure us that they will swiftly reestablish respect for democracy and the law. And, if the United Nations does its job, those greenbacks in Europe boycotting our wood products will be sent away for a long time, too. We will no longer tolerate foreigners who think that what we and other countries do to our forests is any concern of theirs. Let them tell us what happened to their trees before they tell us what we should do with ours. Sherwood Forest was under the protection of the King all along, and there isn't a tree of it left.

Do not be misled by the desperate arguments of the radical environmental left. Some will compare our logging practices with the practices that recently destroyed the eastern fishery. They will say that we are drift-netting the forest. They will claim that the fishing industry went for the last fish even when it knew that such practices would end fishing, and that we are pursuing the same policy in forestry. But let us state as clearly and profoundly as possible that a tree is not a fish, and never will be. We have never seen a menu offer cedar cutlets, fillets of fir or spruce and chips nor do we expect to. We take one large section of the forest at a time and remove everything in it. Now what has that got to do with drift-netting? Finally, in fishing it is true that taking the last fish was devastating to the eastern fishery, but when we come to the last tree it will still give us enough seeds to create another forest. For this kind of clear information about what is happening in our resource industries you need only read the full page info-ads we place in newspapers and on TV to help readers understand what is really going on. Someone has to correct the vicious accusations that we are not planting a tree for each tree we cut, that we can't successfully replant a forest and that the trees we do farm are so inferior to old-growth trees that they are difficult to market.

The logging industry, however, is not closed-minded. We have demonstrated many times that we will negotiate with anyone on any issue just as long as talking does not interfere with logging. We will even pay for the reports. To keep in touch with unfolding policies, we often appoint forestry officials to our company's board of governors, and we contribute heavily to their forestry institutions, so long as their message to future foresters is not confused but clearcut. And we keep an open line to the newspapers and radio and TV stations where we place our ads, simply to ensure that there is a logical consistency between their point of view on forestry issues and ours.

If anyone still doubts our corporate goodwill, let me repeat the offer forestry companies have made in such situations before: we paid the government twenty-five thousand dollars fair-and-square for the licence to clearcut Stanley Park, but we will be happy to cancel it if we are simply paid the nine million that we would earn from selling the logs. It's our idea of everyone giving a little. What could be fairer than that?

Although many of us who lead multinational logging companies are not British Columbians, we think of this province as our own, and if people watch closely, they will see that we behave as if it is, too. Anyone who doubts that we would treat Stanley Park with care, respect and grace, need only fly over this province to see what we have done in the forests over the years. The malcontents claim we will cut and run, as we have done in other countries, when the most valuable old-growth trees are all gone. But if we get Stanley Park, incredible new logging opportunities become possible throughout this province and this country. We will be partners with the people for years to come, visiting regularly from our offices in New York even in bad weather.

Citizens of B.C., these are your trees; don't let them stand around doing nothing. Wake up! Create jobs, profit and progress. The Japanese are anxious to buy our logs just to store for the future. Don't waste a minute. Let's clearcut Clayoquot Sound today and Stanley Park tomorrow!

## It May Be Law, But Is It Justice?

After our arrest, the Clayoquot experience shifted location from the woods to the courtroom. What began as a confrontation with a logging company removing old-growth rainforest ended up as a confrontation with the Supreme Court of British Columbia over our violation of its injunction. That confrontation became critical when we were informed that the charge against us had been raised from civil to criminal contempt. If we were found guilty we faced fines, jail, community service and the possibility of a criminal record. With a criminal record we would be unable to travel to most countries, and that meant that Margot and I would be unable to visit our office in the United States or to keep business engagements abroad, including several already arranged for the coming year. Discussions with other protesters at our arraignment in court and with lawyers who were volunteering their services increased our concern. No promising line of defense was emerging. When Judge Bouck's horrendous sentences for the first group of protesters were announced—45 days in jail and fines up to $1500.00—our concern turned to panic. We began looking for a lawyer.

When we explained our situation and our reasons, the first lawyer we consulted said, "You don't seem to understand; the business of the court is law, not justice. There is only one issue here; whether or not you disobeyed a court injunction—a law—against interfering with MacMillan Bloedel's logging operations in Clayoquot Sound. The police and the company both have you on videotape, and you were both on the evening news. If you were there—and you were—you are guilty of civil contempt; if you flagrantly attracted public attention to your acts—and you did—it's criminal contempt."

We were beginning to feel hopeless. "What can we do?" we asked. "Your defence," he replied, "is either to attack the law itself, or plead guilty and get off with the lightest sentence possible. Challenging the law would cost a great deal of money, and the result would still be in doubt. I think we should argue for a light sentence, take as little of the court's time as possible and get this over with." What would that mean? "First we will plead guilty and present as many character references as possible to show that you are otherwise upstanding citizens. Then we will claim that you were confused and didn't realize what you were doing, that you never intended to show contempt for the law. You will take the stand and apologize to the court for your contemptuous acts and promise that you will never do such a thing again. It is really the only plea that will help you."

But what about the reason we were there, the preservation of the old-growth forests in Clayoquot Sound? "That is your motive," the lawyer told us; "the reason you went to Kennedy River Bridge. The court is only interested in your intent, what your acts were implicitly intended to accomplish. Because you flagrantly attracted attention to your contempt for the law, you must be punished to preserve order and prevent chaos. The trees, the environment, the rights of native people, logging practices like clearcutting, shipping unworked logs abroad may all be important issues, but the court will say that they have nothing to do with these charges and this case." Although our consultant did not end up defending us, he proved to be absolutely right about the court's point of view.

Margot and I pleaded guilty—we were according to the court—and although we neither apologized nor assured the court we would not do such things again, we could say truthfully that we did not act to show contempt for the court. I must admit, however, that, as we experienced the court in action against us, our contempt for its proceedings steadily deepened. We are not lawyers, we cannot argue the law; but as thoughtful citizens, we can argue whether or not we felt unjustly treated.

My first concern was that the court seemed grimly determined to make criminals out of people who were not criminals at all, for deeds that are difficult to characterize as crimes. These people— mostly young people representing many walks of life, most if not all, without any previous record of trouble with the law—went to Clayoquot at their own expense and endured considerable discomfort living on the land, some of them for several summers, for the single purpose of drawing public attention to the massive logging of old-growth rainforests in Clayoquot Sound. Their camp was run in an orderly way and their protest was conducted according to rigorous rules. No intimidation or attack was ever conducted against any person associated with the logging operations; no property was ever damaged or destroyed as part of the protest; no damage to the environment was allowed or any mess or litter left behind. We stayed overnight at the bridge and the next morning where 1000 people had been milling the day before, we could find no trace, not even a cigarette butt. While logging was delayed on a number of occasions, it was never halted, and when anyone was arrested they went with the police without resisting. Above all, not one protester was there for personal gain; no one stood to profit from his or her actions in any way. The outcome they sought was a benefit for the province at large and for future generations.

These are the strangest criminals I have ever met, committing a crime so strange it is difficult to distinguish from an act of citizenship or public service. The government's subsequent attention to Clayoquot and logging proves that the protesters had an important point to make. Why did the authorities not establish a dialogue rather than criminalize worthy young people for attempting to contribute?

Faced with criminalizing non-criminals, the court understandably practised law in a cave, focussed on its own arcane ground without any reference to the world outside or to the critical issues involved. The legal options open to the defendants were severely limited. Applications for a jury trial and requests to call expert witnesses were routinely denied. All arguments based on the peoples' rights protected by the Canadian constitution, all arguments based on precedents in law and in protest, and all arguments based on local and global forest and environmental issues were denied, along with all appeals lodged in a higher B.C. court. It is difficult to feel justice at work in a court of such foregone conclusions. The only issue the court would consider was the insult to its injunction, proven with an interesting update on the Star Chamber, namely, "We turn on the VCR: if your face appears, you are guilty; if it doesn't you are innocent." The protest was about forestry issues of vital concern to the people of this province, but the charge was interpreted so that no forestry issue was ever considered. By restricting all debate to injunction law, the court effectively disarmed the protesters of their strongest and most appropriate defense, eliminated all the significant issues and trivialized proceedings that continued for nearly a year. As a result, the courts spent hundreds of hours and millions of dollars without clarifying a single issue in the debate, except,

"Don't infuriate a Supreme Court judge who has signed an injunction." Law in a cave, far from the world.

What made our situation worse was the feeling that the RCMP, MacMillan Bloedel and the Supreme Court considered it their case against us. Of course, it was the Supreme Court's injunction granted to M&B to be enacted by the RCMP, so they were the front-line triumvirate. Despite their protests to the contrary, the government and the Attorney General's office also appeared to be on the team determined to silence us. I have always believed that the law is scrupulously even-handed and dedicated to protecting the rights of the people in action against those with power and in positions of privilege. It seems that we are the people, but we were on a very steep playing field against very powerful and privileged opponents. There was never a single opportunity for us to prevail; none of us did; and we saw no effort by the courts to ensure that we ever had a glimmer of hope. There is an obscenity in so much power massed to crush citizens with so little. Democracy shudders.

Even if we grant the court its focus on injunction law, we can still argue that we were driven to act by a situation of imminent peril. It seems to me that there are situations where it is essential to violate an injunction, or at least where one can act without obedience to the law as one's first consideration. The following are extreme examples but, as analogies, show the possibility of exception. If the court issued an injunction to keep us at least 200 yards away from a sex offender living in our community, and we violated it to stop him from forcing a young girl into his van, we would, I assume, be praised, not punished by the court. Similarly, if the public were forbidden by injunction from entering a property, but ignored it to save the children inside the house when a fire broke out, they would at least be pardoned on the grounds of imminent peril. This is exactly our case. We did not go to Clayoquot Sound with any thought about violating a court injunction, but rather because of our perception that irreplaceable old-growth is in imminent peril of destruction. Studies conducted before and since the protest confirm that the peril is real.

If we wait for police, the young girl will be gone; if we wait for firemen, the children will be burned alive; and if we wait for legislation or an election, the old-growth in Clayoquot will be cut and shipped. Surely the issue is not, can the court prove we were naughty, but can we prove that we responded to a situation of imminent peril: the loss of threatened, irreplaceable, very valuable old-growth rainforests.

I am also convinced that these judges had no right to try us, that all decisions against us should be reversed and that the court should issue a public apology, on the grounds that accusers cannot fairly judge those they accuse because they have a predisposition to find them guilty. It is not justice when the accuser—the supreme court—sits in judgement of those they have accused—the Clayoquot protesters. The fair judge is not predisposed to find a defendant guilty, but weighs, like Justice herself, innocence or guilt evenly in the balance and is blind to any circumstance or condition that might unfairly tip the scales. The accuser has already declared his prejudice, making him fit to prosecute guilt, but clearly unfit to fairly judge it. But that is only the beginning. These men were not accusing us of violating just any law; they were accusing us of violating a law they created themselves. They had not only a predisposition but a necessity to find the protesters guilty. They had to find us guilty to preserve their power by injunction. Think of it. Someone makes a rule, accuses you of breaking it and then is appointed to judge whether you are innocent or guilty of breaking the rule he has made and accused you of breaking. Not only that, but only by finding you guilty can your judge maintain the authority of the rules he makes. And he is angry at what you have done. If that makes you think of kangaroos, too, you won't be surprised by the final score: Supreme Court judges—630 (at last count); Clayoquot protesters—0.

Even the injunction law we were tried under seems shaky to me. Judge J.A. Middleton of Ontario said that, "Government by injunction is a thing abhorrent to the Law of England and of this Province." He was referring to the fact that by issuing an injunction, a judge is making law where none existed before. Laws normally emanate from legislation passed by elected representatives of the people, not by individual, politically-appointed judges. But there was no law regulating logging, only a forestry code, and no officers of the law to enforce these regulations or laws, if any existed, since foresters can hardly be expected both to work with loggers and to police them. Despite the  evidence that logging companies exceeded allowable cuts, for instance, no charges were laid by foresters. Surely, "exceeding allowable cuts" is a technical way of saying stealing our trees. If anyone gets caught exceeding the allowable shopping they have paid for, they get arrested, and they don't get to keep the goods. Logging companies seriously exceed the allowable cut—apparently they are on a self-monitoring honour system—are caught, but never charged, and get to keep the stolen trees. So technically, the only law of the forests was made by the judge who signed an injunction against the protests. That judge, apparently, made no effort to study the forestry situation or to seek arguments from the protesters, but simply heard the complaint from the company and signed.

Surely it is time to take this power to make temporary legislation away from judges in cases of public dispute. They do not represent the people or follow a democratic decision-making process. Let us instead assign legislation by injunction to a legislative committee responsible to the province and its citizens. This shabby, so-called law that had to be defended at all costs is an outrage to any thoughtful person and should be an embarrassment to the judiciary. Only royalty and tyrants have the power to make arbitrary law and then stomp on the people who will not obey it. My lord, the judge, does not quite qualify.

After we had been sentenced, we returned to court in support of two colleagues from the University of British Columbia whose cases were to be heard. During the proceedings, Jessica Michalofsky's name was called. She rose and said something close to the following: "My Lord, I cannot afford a lawyer so I will defend myself." She was tall, self-assured, simply dressed and had her hair cut short. "I plead guilty to criminal contempt. I went to Clayoquot to preserve the old-growth forest. I did not go to show contempt for the law, but I'm not sorry I went either, and I cannot promise that I will never do such a thing again." The judge asked how he should sentence her. She replied, "I am a student at college and cannot afford a fine; I live in too remote a place for electronic monitoring so I will have to take a jail sentence. I would like to begin it right away because I have a job tree planting that begins in three weeks." My wife and I were impressed by her quiet strength and clarity. The judge was in a quandary; this was no criminal, and he, like us, would be proud to have her as a daughter. "Can't you suggest any alternatives?" he asked with concern, but she couldn't and was sentenced to six days in jail with nine months probation added to deter her from further "criminal" activity.

When the country begins to devour its strong and dedicated young people, it is in great need of deep reflection, a rededication of purpose and some dramatic changes in process. Fortunately, young people like Jessica can take great pride in the significant changes their protest has already wrought in forestry practice in this province since August, 1993: a new and tougher forestry code, much stiffer fines against companies that violate logging regulations, a prohibition against exporting whole logs, increased payments from companies for logging our trees and the Vancouver Island Core Report extending the amount of protected old-growth forest. It is easy to see these developments as admissions that the protesters were right all along, and that their action drew attention to an outrage in our forests. Outrage happens and we should be both reassured and grateful that Jessica Michalofsky, and many people like her, are ready to stand up and be counted whenever it does. Jessica's trial for C-Day was on the fiftieth anniversary of D-Day.

## *To Our Children's Children's Children*

If you find some faded photograph
Of your great-great grandmother and me,

Remember us as two who could not sit at home
While earth's rare ancient forests
Were cut down at Clayoquot Sound,
But went with a thousand others to protest.
Hushed dark in camp, our cars and trucks
In dusty column through somber woods,
We gathered at the bridge they had to cross.
Dawn broke as we built our frail blockade;
Drums beat, banners unfurled, a circle
Of women danced and chanted as young and old
Hugged their friends then sat upon the road.
Newscopters clacking overhead, we waved
And sang, over and over, louder and louder;
   "We won't take it any more;
   We are stronger than before!
   We won't take it any more;
   We are stronger than before!"
Then whispers: "Stay on the road; they can't arrest
Us all." "It's nine o'clock and no trees are falling
In Clayoquot Sound." "No one is working today;
We've won." "Listen! O my god, here they come..."
Cop cars, logging trucks, speaker vans
And paddy wagons broke from the bush,
Rolling at us, sitting side by side, holding
Hands, waiting for what came next, our arrest.

*Clayoquot, Walbran, Tatshenshini...*
*Kitlope, Carmanah and Stikine.*

If we failed, your heritage is gone:
Great spires of hemlock, cedar, spruce and fir
Rising for a thousand years two hundred feet
Or more, so huge that fifteen hikers linking
Hands could not reach around their trunks;
And when sun-shafts fell through latticed branches
Into those great-columned chapel groves, even

Non-believers felt a radiant presence in the vast
Closeness of their quiet and eternal calm.
We assumed such forests were protected
And preserved for you: treasury of medicines
Yet unknown; home to species, many never seen before
Source of work, forever, if we hewed the timber
Here we shipped abroad; this wonder to a planet
Longing for the very wilderness so many nations
Long ago consumed; this pulsing heart of nature,
This breath; this Gaia, gone, and gone once, forever
Gone from earth. Forgive us. There seemed so much,
And suddenly there was so little ancient forest left:

*Clayoquot, Walbran, Tatshenshini...*
*Kitlope, Carmanah and Stikine.*

These great trees—hear them coming down—
Are not the people's, and there seems no way
To get them back to save. The party we elected
Promised to preserve the very wilderness
They gave away to companies they have joined.
What can we do? They are too strong when they
Conspire: government, corporation, the police;
And now our last resort, the court, has turned
On us; we may be done: criminal contempt,
Mass trial with no delays, and sentences
To silence us. But we aren't finished yet;
Laws protect rights, not privileges for a few;
Courts preserve justice, not power. If they treat
People with contempt, they are through.
Power tramples native history, fouls thriving
Fisheries, smashes wild habitats, devastates
The countryside and ships our wealth abroad,
All with impunity. We sat upon a road to stop
A crime. After sixty years of lawful life,
We sat upon a road. Time comes for everyone

To make a choice, to act; the time has come
To take our forests back.

*Clayoquot, Walbran, Tatshenshini...*
*Kitlope, Carmanah and Stikine.*

So if you will remember us, go to Clayoquot Sound;
See for yourself if ancient trees still tower there,
Or some stone monument to "the greatest temperate
Rainforest ever seen on earth" now stands in a sea
Of burned-out stumps on a clearcut mountainside.
Then count the multinationals who reaped and ran,
And who still harvest trees in ways they always can.
See Kennedy River Bridge and remember we sat there
With a thousand others in the summer of nineteen
ninety-three;
And if you would honour us, choose some value greater
Than yourselves for a future better than today,
Then stand up for it and be not moved. So you keep
Us alive. With love from your great, great grandmother
And me from long ago...we remain forever in...

*Clayoquot, Walbran, Tatshenshini...*
*Kitlope, Carmanah and Stikine.*
*Clayoquot, Walbran, Tatshenshini...*
*Kitlope, Carmanah and Stikine.*

### References

Bay, Christian, and Walker, Charles C. *Civil Disobedience: Theory and Practice.* Montreal: Black Rose Books, 1975.

*Canadian Charter of Rights: Annotated.* Aurora (Ont.): Canada Law Book, 1992.

Carson, Rachel. *Silent Spring.* Boston: Houghton Mifflin, 1962.

Gibbons, Maurice. *Toward a Universal Curriculum for a Global Generation.* Vancouver: World Citizens for a Global Generation, 1979.

Hogg, Peter W. *Constitutional Law of Canada.* (3rd Edition) Scarborough (Ont.): Carswell, 1992.

Jensen, Vickie. *Where the People Gather: Carving a Totem Pole.* Vancouver: Douglas and McIntyre, 1992.

Kimmins, Hamish. *Balancing Act: Environmental Issues in Forestry.* Vancouver: UBC Press, 1992.

Lyons, C.P. *Trees, Shrubs and Flowers to Know in British Columbia.* Toronto: J.M. Dent, 1974.

McKibben, Bill. *The End of Nature.* New York: Doubleday, 1989.

Myers, Dr. Norman, (Ed.). *Gaia: An Atlas of Planet Management.* New York: Doubleday, 1984.

Nelson, Joyce. "Pulp and Propaganda." *The Canadian Forum,* (July-August, 1994), pp. 14-19.

*An Old Growth Strategy for British Columbia.* Victoria: Ministry of Forests, c. 1992.

Ornstein, Robert, and Ehrlich, Paul. *New World New Mind: Moving Toward Consciousness Evolution.* New York: Simon and Schuster, 1989.

Pike, Graham, and Selby, David. *Global Teacher, Global Learner.* London (UK): Hodder and Stoughton, 1988.

*The Sierra Report.* (13:2). Summer, 1994.

Stewart, Hilary. *Cedar: Tree of Life to the Northwest Coast Indians.* Vancouver: Douglas and McIntyre, 1984.

Stoltmann, Randy. *Hiking Guide to the Big Trees of Southwestern British Columbia.* (Second Ed.) Vancouver: Western Canada Wilderness Committee, 1991.

Vance, Joan E. *Tree Planning: A Guide to Public Involvement in Forest Stewardship.* Vancouver: B.C. Public Interest Advocacy Centre, 1990.

World Commission on Environment and Development. *Our Common Future.* Oxford: Oxford University Press, 1987.

# The Clayoquot Show Trials

RONALD B. HATCH

Over the Clayoquot summer of 1993, people came to the Kennedy River Bridge on the west coast of Vancouver Island in their thousands. People came from Germany, Australia, the U.S., Poland, Mexico and all the Canadian provinces. They came to protest the provincial government's decision to allow MacMillan Bloedel to clearcut the irreplaceable ancient temperate rainforest. The summer 1993 protest against clearcutting was by no means the first; protests had been occurring on a smaller scale for about a decade.[1] But it was the NDP government's April 13, 1993, decision to allow substantial clearcut logging in the Clayoquot that caused people to protest in massive numbers. During the summer, approximately 900 people chose to be arrested in these protests. Following the principles of civil disobedience, they chose to break a small law—in this case, a court injuction—in order to stop a large injustice. While expecting to pay a penalty for disobeying the court injunction, those arrested also expected to be treated fairly by their police force and their courts. By the time the last mass trials were winding down (and this is happening while I write in the summer of 1994: one year after the 1993 protests began), few of the Clayoquot supporters believed that they had been treated fairly. The trials confirmed their opinion that the courts and the government were the handmaidens of the trans-national logging companies. Indeed, I think it is fair to say that no one—and that includes lawyers, judges, defendants, the police, government officials, the ordinary citizen— was happy with the way the courts handled Clayoquot.

When such large numbers of people believe that the courts failed in dealing with the Clayoquot, a discussion of the trials becomes imperative. It may appear presumptuous for someone like myself, untrained in the law, to undertake such an analysis. But the people who can give the best legal explanation will not—at least in public. Numerous lawyers and even some judges have told me privately that the court's handling of the Clayoquot trials should be critically evaluated. But lawyers are generally reluctant to criticize publicly judges and the legal system. For that matter, so are junior judges, since such criticism could affect their careers. For this reason, the judicial system has received relatively little criticism over the years. If there is going to be an examination of the Clayoquot trials, it must come from someone outside the legal/judicial system. And, for all my lack of legal training, I have one major advantage: I am a Clayoquot "arrestee" myself. I know what it feels like to be swallowed up by the court system and spewed out the other end as a "criminal."

My one concern when I began this essay was of being once again found in contempt of court. Judges are very prickly about their domain, and a number of them have warned people away from criticizing the trials. Mr. Justice Spencer has said, rather ominously, that people should criticize "quietly."[2] One can take comfort, however, in the thought that citizens have the right, even the responsibility, to criticize their institutions—even the courts and their "lordships."

The question, then, is where to begin, for the issues surrounding the trials are enormously complex. In the course of this paper I shall be dealing with a number of large issues: the appropriateness of injunctions in cases of civil disobedience, the background to the charge of criminal contempt, and the role of the Attorney General and the government. While it is tempting to address these issues directly, I believe that this would be a mistake, for it would omit the experience of the protestors in the trials. To adopt legal language at the outset is to adopt the very language of the judges. In the Clayoquot trials, the judges repeated over and over: "If you were on the road, and knowingly disobeyed the injunction, then you are guilty. That is the law." Yet if that is all there is to it, why then did so many people feel ill-served? After all, the protestors came from many walks of life, and many of them struggled hard to understand what was happening to them. They came away convinced the trials were unfair. In order to reach into this primary experience of ordinary people before the law—something that judges and academic experts in the law often ignore—we need to examine what it felt like to be an honourable protestor/an alleged contemnor.

The best place to begin is with the mass trials themselves. The Clayoquot mass trials, as they came to be called. Of the tens of thousands of protestors who travelled to Clayoquot Sound, over 900 were arrested, over 860 were eventually brought to trial.[3] Because of the large numbers of people on trial, the courts decided at the beginning to hurry people through. At one point, there was even the possibility that all the Clayoquot supporters arrested on August 9th (some 250) would be tried in a single large hall in Victoria, with teams of prosecutors working to finish in a short time.[4] Thankfully, wiser heads put a stop to this suggestion.

Even when the trials were broken down into smaller groups, there were still major problems, and at times one was left with the impression that the courts wanted "show trials"—trials meant to "show" the public the harsh results of dissent, but which did not deal with the fundamental issues. The first trial included 44 defendants. At the time, the court (or, as was often the case—the Crown/court—since the two frequently became a single entity) maintained that it was possible to give each individual within the group an individual trial and still speed up the procedure by calling the evidence for everyone in the group at one time. The Crown justified this approach, claiming similarity of evidence, even though defendants, coming from diverse places, had protested on different days at different times. The defendants were treated as a group when it was necessary to prove the principle of _criminal contempt_ (in other words, "an open, continuous and flagrant defiance of a court order"[5]), but the Crown reverted to the individual when it was again convenient for prosecutorial purposes.

Because the court had started out with the notion that all the Clayoquot supporters could be tried _en masse_, when it later decided to offer so-called "individual" trials within groups of 20, 30 or 40 people, they still retained the earlier idea that the individuals before them were in fact a single, large group. As a result, the trials became incredibly confusing. Mr. Justice Bouck at one point confessed: "we are sort of allowed to make the rules as they [the trials] go along...."[6] As is well known, interpretation of the law is based on precedent or preceding decisions in similar cases or circumstances. The idea that a judge was making up the rules as he went along is abhorrent to the whole idea of law within a democratic society. But that is what occurred.

In the Clayoquot trials, the court treated the defendants before them as a group or as individuals—as it pleased the court. A good example of this convenient confusion can be seen in the procedures of the later trials. Often a defendant would raise a point, only to be told that it had already been dealt with in a previous trial. Or, a judge would begin a trial by saying that he did not want to hear all the same "stuff" that had been presented in earlier trials. "I am bound by my brother judge" was a comment that one heard repeatedly in the trials. Clearly the Clayoquot defendants were not receiving individual trials. To administer an individual trial, the judge has to look at all the evidence. He cannot pretend that the trial in front of him is an extension of previous trials. The judge did not preside at the earlier trial. He did not hear the evidence; he did not know the circumstances. And certainly the defendants did not know that their evidence had already been dealt with. For the judge to pretend that he had heard the evidence, meant that he was treating the current defendant as if he were the same as the previous one. This confusion over whether the defendants were being seen as a group or as individuals persisted to the end.

That the court only pretended to offer the Clayoquot supporters an individual trial within larger groups became evident again in the way the court treated individuals in their struggle to be involved. As the date for trials drew near, people wrote, phoned and faxed the court co-ordinator, asking to be advised of pre-trial meetings and requesting to be involved. No response. Instead, dates were announced and the protestors were issued orders to attend. When questioned about this failure to involve the individuals, the court replied that it could not possibly respond to so many people as individuals. But such a reply implicitly admits that the individual defendants were being seen as a group and treated as a group.

In the beginning when the trial dates were being set, the Crown/court set the dates according to the Crown/court's calendar without the normal consultation with defendant's lawyers. This made it virtually impossible for the defendants to have the legal counsel they had chosen. In a normal trial, the Crown Counsel and the defendant's lawyer meet together and reach an agreement on an appropriate date for the trial, taking into account the court schedule. But in the first trial, people were told to appear on the given date, no matter what their situations were or what their lawyers had suggested about dates. At one point the Crown Counsel declared the issues were straightforward and there was no need for legal representation.[7] One would have expected the judge to explode in anger at such a claim. Instead, he tacitly agreed. Presumably the reasoning was that the defendants were already guilty. Certainly they were all found guilty. The point needs to be emphasized: no one in the Clayoquot trials was found not-guilty of criminal contempt, unless there was a technical error with the trial procedure. Nor was anyone found guilty of civil contempt. A perfect score for the court!

The presumption of guilt on the part of the judges infuriated many of the defendants. If they were already guilty, then why go through the charade of the trial? As will be seen presently, this presumption of guilt is implicit in the very nature of contempt of court.

When the case was appealed by a number of lawyers acting for the Clayoquot supporters, the B.C. Appeal Court Judges did not agree that the defendants were denied legal counsel, nor that their rights were compromised during the process.[8] Fortunately, however, the judges in later trials saw the *menetekel:* they quietly made it possible for defendants to obtain adjournments and eased the way for them to obtain appropriate legal counsel. In other words, although the Appeal Court refused to admit an error had been made, later judges scrambled to correct the error. For the Appeal Court to admit the error would have meant reversing the decision by Mr. Justice Bouck. But by the time the Appeal Court heard the case, many of the people tried by Mr. Justice Bouck had already served their time in jail. Embarrassing? Fear of possible lawsuits?

Yet another point about the large group trials was the manner in which judges tended to tar all of the defendants with the same brush. For example, if one defendant said something out of order, or behaved improperly, the judge growled at the entire group of individuals. In some of the trials there were so many Clayoquot supporters in the dock that the judge did not know all their identities. Therefore, remarks from the public were often attributed to defendants who then suffered the adverse consequences. The transcript of the first trial is liberally scattered with questions by "Unidentified Speaker,"[9] who may or may not have been a defendant. Not knowing the people in front of him, the judge did not know who made which comments, and he became annoyed with them all. The facade of an individual trial became apparent. To their credit, most of the defendants kept their sense of humour and used the trial situation to defend themselves as well as they could. They could not be blamed if occasionally they became despondent or cynical. At one point during this series of trials, a Crown Counsel asked a defendant how things were going. "Not so good," was the response. "Oh," replied the Crown Counsel, "did you see the kangaroo hopping through the courtroom?"[10]

This from the Crown!

A consistent request made by most of the Clayoquot defendants was trial by jury. Each time it was denied. Trial by jury may seem a small point, but in such cases (Order by Injunction) the judiciary is the offended party; the judiciary makes the findings of fact; the judiciary interprets the laws; the judiciary decides on guilt or innocence. And in the Clayoquot trials, the "offence" did not take place in their presence. There is no other circumstance in law where the offended party is the judge *and* jury *and* passes sentence on his being offended. In some cases, the judge who had made or extended the original injunction was asked to rule on that injunction. Judges claimed that they could be objective in such cases, that there was no need for a jury trial. It was, however, apparent to many observers that some of the judges reacted emotionally to the breaking of their court order and did not remain the independent arbiters of justice that we expect.

Indeed, when the case was appealed, Richard Peck, a prominent Vancouver lawyer, examined the origins of contempt trials in Britain. He pointed out that, historically, contempt trials were conducted with juries.[11] In part, this was because the offence was serious. The Clayoquot defendants were charged with *criminal* contempt of court. And *criminal* contempt, unlike other offences, does not specify a maximum sentence. Juries were also used in the past because it was deemed inappropriate for a judge to judge himself. Peck's appeal, however, was denied. The judges decided that their fellow judges could be fair. But would they be seen to be fair?

\* \* \*

Although much more could be said about the difficulties caused by the mass trials, let us now turn to a different aspect of the issue: the actual offence, or alleged offence, in the trials. Even after the protestors (or "protectors," as they were sometimes called) had swallowed the insult of the mass trials with no counsel and no jury, they had great difficulties in making sense of the "crime" they were supposed to have committed—criminal contempt. What a strange crime it was in the circumstances. They were not in court for blocking the road and stopping MacMillan Bloedel from clearcutting the Clayoquot rainforest, but for insulting the court. And for doing it in a "criminal" manner.

Moreover, once the first trial was underway, it was apparent to everyone concerned that the courts were uncertain how to try criminal contempt. Most readers will probably find it hard to believe that the courts did not understand their own business, but observers at the trial were soon convinced that the trials became a living Kafkaesque spectacle. Looking at the trials with hindsight, commentators have sometimes tended to conclude that the confusion arose because the Clayoquot defendants were often unrepresented and did not understand the law. Certainly the defendants were frequently bewildered by the court procedures. They were sometimes unsure when to speak and how. Yet that is not the point. They assumed that the courts would/could explain the "charge" levelled against them and they kept pressing for a full explanation.

The confusion over the "charge" and the way to handle the procedures for dealing with it arose because of the curious nature of criminal contempt. Because criminal contempt was treated in these cases as a Common Law offense, and was therefore not under the Criminal Code (although in fact there is another provision for criminal contempt of court under the Criminal Code) there was no "charge" as such. Yet this was not explained in court, and frequently the judges forgot the point themselves, so used were they to dealing with a "charge."

The Clayoquot defendants were at a loss to understand the charge-that-was-no-charge, which had brought them to court. If there was no charge, then they could plead neither guilty nor not-guilty. What were they supposed to do? they asked. The judge refused to answer, but then went on to allow different sorts of pleas, even though there was no "charge" and such pleas were absurd under the circumstances. Throughout the trials, this plea-taking was permitted, nay, invited, even though it made absolutely no sense in the case of contempt.

Still worse, when the Clayoquot defendants requested information on their crime, the judges sometimes gave contradictory information or refused to offer information. The transcripts are full of this style of questioning and response. In the very first trial, that held under Mr. Justice Bouck, the Clayoquot defendants—still under the impression that there must be a "charge"—demanded to *see* the charge in black and white. None could be produced. When the Crown Counsel found himself at a loss, the learned Judge finally decided that he would help out by drafting something that could serve as a charge.[12] This was incredible! I can hardly believe it even now as I try to explain. And yet the transcript speaks for itself. The judge, who is supposed to be an impartial arbiter between two parties (in this case he was a party), stepped in and drew up a "sort of" charge: what he called a "Complaint." He even suggested that the Crown Counsel and the defendants and their lawyers might get together and study it. In all fairness, he did this to be helpful. But what it showed was that the judges appeared not to know the procedures. Either that, or there were no defined procedural rules.

In the end, the Crown Counsel did not accept the "charge" as drawn up by Mr. Justice Bouck, but no other solution was offered or accepted. And the trials continued. Some of the Clayoquot defendants argued that a mistrial must have occurred, yet through it all Crown Counsel and the judges steered the trial so that the procedural matters were never resolved. If the problem had been only with the Clayoquot supporters not understanding the law, as some have thought, then one would expect that eventually the courts would get their act together and sort out the problems surrounding criminal contempt. Not so. The confusions continue to proliferate. Because the "charge" of criminal contempt was never clarified, probation orders and the like continue to be made out incorrectly.[13] And court officials seem not to know enough, or have enough authority to correct the problem.

Why was there such confusion over criminal contempt? Part of the answer is that criminal contempt of court is not a frequent charge, and some of the judges who presided over the case had little or no experience of dealing with it. They had learned their trade as lawyers and had rarely encountered it during that stage of their careers. Another reason why there was such confusion is that the "contempt" in these cases did not take place in the courtroom, but at Kennedy River Bridge. Contempt of court, as it is usually understood, is applied to someone who is disrespectful in the courtroom in the "face of the judge." There is no doubt that judges need to be able to maintain order in their courtrooms, and if a person before them is contemptuous, they need to be able to find them in contempt. And they do so immediately. But in the Clayoquot trials, where the alleged contempt took place *ex facie* (out of the face of the judge), this meant that the entire trial procedure was far more complicated.

To see just how complicated it became (and how confused the judges became), one needs to understand how the contempt charges developed and were applied in British Columbia. The protests against the bad logging practices had begun in the late 1980s. The procedure was that once a protest began, the logging companies filed civil suits against the environmentalists. After having filed the civil suit, the companies were then allowed to file for a court injunction against protesters—while they prepared themselves for a future trial date. If individuals broke the court order, they were then arrested for contempt of court and brought to trial. The companies soon discovered that it was much easier to have the injunctions extended than it was to go through the bother of a civil suit. Consequently, they did this, and worked through the injunction to have the environmentalists charged for contempt.

As the years rolled on in the battle between the environmentalists and the clearcutters, and the protests did not cease, the judges found that they were being asked for more and more injunctions. The environmentalists were finding increasing numbers of proven bad logging practices—practices which destroyed salmon spawning in most watersheds; caused massive soil displacement on steep slopes, compromising reforestry efforts, etc.

The protests continued to grow. In such circumstances, one might have thought that the judges would begin to question the validity of injunctions, or wonder about the reason for public protest, or even ask why the companies were not proceeding with their civil suits. But no, as one reads the judges' "reasons for judgement," it becomes evident that they became ever more distressed at the public's failure to recognize their orders, and they reacted by increasing their sentences.

The other development with the charge of contempt was predictable. In the early years, the judges had found the protestors guilty of civil contempt. When the protests did not cease, the judges slowly raised civil contempt to criminal contempt. From reading the transcripts and "Reasons for Judgement" from 1990 onwards, one can observe that the judges were not all that clear on what criminal contempt signified. The judges frequently refer to the "charge" of criminal contempt, almost as if it were under the Criminal Code, and not under Common Law.[14] Moreover, they seemed unclear whether there were two separate charges: the first, civil, and the second, criminal. Or, if there were only one charge of contempt—with the judge being left to decide whether to choose civil or criminal contempt. In one case, Madam Justice Saunders noted that the defendants were charged with criminal contempt, but then added that she must find if they were guilty of criminal or civil contempt.[15] In another case, that presided over by Chief Justice Esson himself, he decided to cover all the bases and found that the environmentalists were guilty of *both* civil and criminal contempt.[16]

Then, on July 23, 1992, *and at the request of the plaintiff, MacMillan Bloedel,* Mr. Justice Drost decided to make an order "declaring the contempt proceedings herein to be criminal in nature...."[17] In other words, those breaking the injunction would no longer be tried for "contempt," with the judge having the option to find for civil or criminal. Instead, the charge would be "criminal contempt" at the outset. Looking back on the history of contempt, the courts have tended to say that Mr. Justice Drost's decision was a watershed for the change from civil to criminal contempt, although in fact Mr. Justice Gow treated at least one later case as civil contempt.[18] Moreover, Mr. Justice Drost did not say—so far as I can tell—that all later cases should be treated as criminal contempt, although that is the way the courts chose to view the matter.[19]

This upping of the ante to criminal contempt meant that things were becoming serious. Because the offence was "criminal," it looked as though the Attorney General's office should become involved, since it is the Attorney General's office, through his Crown Counsel, that prosecutes under the Criminal Code. It is interesting to watch the way the trials over the next year began increasingly to have the Attorney General as the prosecutor, although one sometimes finds a trial in which criminal contempt is at issue and there is no Attorney General.[20] The entire question of whether the Crown has to be invited to intervene or whether it can simply take over the case was being canvassed as early as September of 1991.[21]

By this time the whole situation surrounding contempt was extremely complex and muddled. In the beginning, the cases of contempt had not only been treated as _civil contempt_, but they were also in the _civil style of proceeding_. By this, I mean that if one looks at the trial situation, one finds the plaintiff on one side (usually MacMillan Bloedel and their lawyers) and the defendants (the environmentalists, with or without lawyers) on the other. But gradually as the charge moved up from civil contempt to criminal contempt, Crown Counsel makes his appearance. It is still a civil suit in theory—the plaintiff is still MacMillan Bloedel— but MacMillan Bloedel's lawyers are no longer conducting the case. Nor are they present in the court. Instead, there is a Crown Counsel who is prosecuting for the Attorney General's office. What we have here is a mishmash of two types of law: it is criminal because the Attorney General is prosecuting, but it is also civil, because we have a plaintiff and defendants. Moreover, it turns out that contempt is generally treated under Common Law, not as a Criminal Code of Canada offence.[22]

Because the process had grown in this ad hoc fashion, like Topsy, one has the impression that no one truly understood the implications. Once the Clayoquot trials began, however, the hidden contradictions exploded. When the judge was unsure, he tended to ask the prosecutor. They would confer, the Crown would suggest a direction and the judge would defer. As one might expect, the Clayoquot defendants became more and more upset by the seemingly arbitrary nature of the proceedings. Moreover, because they were often unrepresented by lawyers, they asked fundamental questions, to which there were no answers. The emperor, they discovered, had no clothes.

It should be emphasized that in their questioning, the Clayoquot defendants were not being obstreperous, as is sometimes claimed; they were simply trying to understand what they were "charged" with, and they did not receive much help from the judges who were themselves confused. For example, one of the first practical questions the defendants asked was whether they would be left with a permanent criminal record as a result of being found guilty of criminal contempt. If so, then they might well have difficulties in obtaining visas, finding jobs in sensitive areas, etc. A number of the Clayoquot supporters were also planning to study law, and a criminal record would make it difficult to be called to the Bar. As well, they wanted to know if their names would appear on CPIC, the police computer.[23] At first, the consensus was that they would have permanent criminal records, but then it was pointed out that the charges were under Common Law, not the Criminal Code, and thus perhaps they would not. On the other hand, the very name "criminal contempt" caused the judges to forget that the offence was not under the Criminal Code, and they sometimes referred to criminal contempt as an "indictable offence," which implied it was under the Criminal Code.[24] Unable to clarify such questions, the judges were forced into the unusual situation of writing into their judgements that there should be no criminal record, that the criminal contempt conviction would be expunged once the sentence was served, the fines paid, the community hours worked. Yet as Mr. Justice Lambert pointed out in his Appeal decision, the courts cannot tell the police how to handle their records.[25] The court's confusion over this simple matter still haunts the Corrections Service. One suspects that the judges, through their ignorance, may have given a "life sentence," in that they have created problems that will haunt the Clayoquot supporters for life.

Even the question of whether the defendants, the so-called "contemnors," were criminals found no easy response. After all, we were all found guilty of criminal contempt. Does that not make us criminals? Yes, we are criminals, but only until we have finished serving our sentences or paid our fines. As one of the guards at Vancouver Pre-trial put it, with a laugh, as he typed my particulars into the computer: "You're a criminal!" And then he added, "You're a criminal until July 27th, when you will have served your sentence." After that, there is no criminal record, although of course everyone recognizes that the police never erase their records completely.

As has been seen, a major source of confusion arose because the Clayoquot supporters were tried for *criminal contempt*, but not under the *Criminal Code*. Mr. Justice Hutchison, who presided over a number of cases, became so frustrated with the problems caused by the distinctions that he suggested a new term should be invented for criminal contempt, one that replaced "criminal" with some other word such as "exaggerated" or "serious."[26] Yet to make such a suggestion is disingenuous: criminal contempt is called "criminal" precisely because it is a serious criminal offence that brings with it serious jail sentences. It almost seemed as though the judge were suggesting that the Clayoquot supporters should have been tried on a different charge—a suggestion that they could readily have accepted.

Perhaps the question that most plagued the trials and resulted in the most confusion was—who was responsible for the trial? On the courthouse bulletin boards announcing the Clayoquot trials, the trials were registered as MacMillan Bloedel vs Sheila Simpson....[27] Yet there was no MacMillan Bloedel lawyer in the courtroom. Instead, there was a prosecutor, a Crown Counsel from the Attorney General's office. Even to those defendants with no knowledge of the law, it seemed obvious that there was something wrong here. Sheila Simpson and the other people listed had not been involved for a considerable time; they were not there. Neither was MacMillan Bloedel. Still, whenever the Court Clerk called each of the trials in the courtroom it was always called as MacMillan Bloedel versus Sheila Simpson et al. Judges tried vainly to explain that the Crown had taken over the prosecution from MacMillan Bloedel. The Crown had done so because the Crown prosecutes in cases of criminal contempt. Yet if the Crown were prosecuting, why then had the courts not removed MacMillan Bloedel's name and replaced it with that of the Crown? Was there not a major error in the trial procedure? Who was in charge of the case? Who was responsible for the "charge" of criminal contempt? Was it MacMillan Bloedel?—MacMillan Bloedel was said to be the plaintiff. Was it the Crown?—the Crown was certainly prosecuting. Or, was it the Court itself which had "invited" the Crown to intervene?—certainly the judges seemed assured of the defendants' guilt before the trial began. It was all very mysterious. Time and again, the Clayoquot defendants asked for an explanation. None was forthcoming.

More confusion developed when the Clayoquot defendants asked about the Crown Counsel in the courtroom. The Attorney General's office has two types of prosecutors, those for civil cases and those for criminal cases. The criminal prosecutors prosecute the Criminal Code offences. As has been seen, the Clayoquot cases were not being tried under the Criminal Code. The injunctions were civil remedies. Yet the defendants were facing Crown prosecutors from the criminal division of the Attorney General's office.

A greater problem surfaced when it came time for the Clayoquot supporters to argue their cases, and they found that the judges were interested in only two questions: Were you on the road?—Yes. Were you aware of the injunction?—Yes. Guilty!! In other words, the Clayoquot supporters could provide no defence for alleged criminal contempt. How could this be?

To understand the judges' position on criminal contempt, one needs to understand the legal precedent on which they relied. As was mentioned earlier, the law is supposed to build from one case to another, with earlier cases setting precedents for later cases. For Clayoquot, the case that was trotted out over and over was the Supreme Court of Canada's 1992 decision in "United Nurses of Alberta versus Alberta (Attorney General)."[28]

While it is not my intention to turn this essay into an excursion on case law, it is essential to offer a brief summary of the Alberta Nurses case. Originally heard in Alberta, the case involved the Nurses Union and the Alberta Labour Relations Board. The Board directed the Union to stop strike activity. When it refused to desist, the Board had the court issue a court injunction. When the Union still failed to comply, the Attorney General filed a motion that the Union be held in criminal contempt. In December 1991, the Union took the case all the way to the Supreme Court of Canada where the Supreme Court's majority decision held that the Union was in criminal contempt.

The Supreme Court decision on the Alberta Nurses case was then used as the definitive precedent in the Clayoquot situation. The case, one notes, had been decided only a year before the Clayoquot summer, and it was fresh in the judges' minds. In fact, the judgement on the Alberta Nurses case seemed to solve the problem of defining criminal contempt for the judiciary. Prior to this Supreme Court decision, there had been grave difficulties in defining criminal contempt.[29]

But was it an appropriate precedent in this case? There are major differences between the two situations. In the first place, the Clayoquot supporters were not members of a union, nor were they members of a common organization. They paid no dues. They elected no president. They were individuals who had come to Clayoquot from all over the world. The loose association, Friends of Clayoquot Sound, had originally organized the Peace Camp along the highway in the vicinity of the logging sites. The camp served as an information centre for tourists and environmentalists. But most defendants were not connected to it or, for that matter, to any organization, environmental or otherwise.

The Clayoquot defendants then pointed out that the Supreme

Court of Canada had ruled in the Alberta Nurses case that the *Union* was guilty of criminal contempt, but that in the Clayoquot situation, they were being charged individually. There is a major difference here. In the one case—that of the Union—there was an organization that directed all activities. In the Clayoquot case, there was no organization. The Union received a fine; none of its members went to jail. In the Clayoquot case, individuals went to jail. Despite these differences, the ruling against the Union was applied to each individual Clayoquot defendant. Although the discrepancy was pointed out in all the trials, the Crown/court persisted in regarding each Clayoquot defendant as "a sort of" union.

Because of the nature of court precedents, the Crown Counsel also relied on the language of the Alberta Nurses case to describe the Clayoquot supporters. In that case, Supreme Court Justice McLachlin had argued that "To establish criminal contempt the Crown must prove beyond a reasonable doubt that the accused disobeyed or defied a court order in a public way with intent, knowledge or recklessness that the public disobedience will tend to depreciate the authority of the court."[30] And these were the words that the Crown Counsel applied throughout to the Clayoquot defendants. It was their "intent" to defame the court. They had "knowledge" that their actions would depreciate the court's authority. They had behaved with "recklessness" to undermine the authority of the court. With these sorts of allegations being made, one can understand how people felt besmirched after the trial. They had come to Clayoquot Sound to protest the NDP government's Land Use Decision that allowed clearcut logging in the last major stand of ancient temperate rainforest, and the judges were telling them that they had come expressly to insult the court. The Clayoquot defendants felt insulted. And, if I may say so, angry. Their good intentions, their good name, both had been stripped from them by their own courts. As well, the courts had taken a major issue—the clearcutting of our forests—and had turned it into a self-serving concern.

Another reason why it is important to understand the Supreme

Court's decision on the Alberta Nurses case is that the Court introduced some new elements to the concept of criminal contempt. For the first time with criminal contempt, Madam Justice McLachlin had introduced the idea of "intention." Using her reasoning, it was essential for future court judges to deal with the defendant's intentions in defying the Court Order. Yet having introduced the crucial idea of the defendant's intent, Madam Justice McLachlin also seemed to say that judges could tell if an activity was criminal contempt simply by looking at the externals of the situation. As she said in her decision: "the necessary mens rea [state of mind] may be _inferred_ from the circumstances" (my emphasis)."[31] Of course, intention _may_ be inferred from the circumstances. That is pretty standard criminal law. Judges always look at the circumstances to help in determining an accused's state of mind. The difference with the Alberta Nurse's case was that Madam Justice McLachlin seemed to leave the door open for something stronger—that "may" means "can." If this were the case, then the defendants were not allowed to give their own version of their intentions.

It was this interpretation—that it was unnecessary to inquire into the defendant's state of mind—that prevailed throughout the Clayoquot trials. In other words, there was no need to ask the defendants if they intended to bring the court into disrepute. If they were on a public road in defiance of the court order, then the court _knew_ that they intended to insult the court; they could deduce it from the circumstances. The judges did not have to prove beyond a reasonable doubt that the defendants had intended to depreciate the authority of the court. The courts inferred from the public nature of the protest that the defendants had gone to Kennedy River Bridge with the intent to bring the court into disrepute.

One and all, the Clayoquot supporters found it preposterous that the court should say it knew they had gone to the Bridge to defame the court when the court was not visible at the Bridge in the midst of MacMillan Bloedel trucks and clearcut forests. It was preposterous that the court should not allow them to give evidence of their individual *mens rea*, their own intentions, their own state of mind. Indeed, it was the opinion of a number of eminent lawyers that McLachlin may have used language that she did not really intend, since it must always be open for defendants to argue that the court is wrong in its inference about their intentions. After all, the very serious charge of criminal contempt was presumably intended for criminal activity in which people set out deliberately, and perhaps violently, to destroy the rule of law. In the case of the Clayoquot supporters, they had practised civil disobedience without a hint of violence.

In the early days of the trial, a number of lawyers such as Glen Orris and Fred Easton held workshops for the Clayoquot supporters and introduced them to the Alberta Nurses precedent. They pointed out that the court, in using the Alberta Nurses case, would attempt to infer the defendant's state of mind or intent, but that it would be open to each defendant to describe his or her own thoughts or state of mind at the Kennedy River Bridge. Moreover, they could then bring into evidence those facts which led them to their beliefs and ultimately to the Kennedy River Bridge. This seemed logical to the Clayoquot supporters in the pre-trial period. After all, they had gone to the Kennedy River Bridge to prevent the clearcutting of Clayoquot. They had not been thinking about impugning the courts.

What the public never understood, and indeed, what most of the defendants could not believe, was that once the trials were under way, the judges ruled out of order any attempt on the defendant's part to discuss or describe their intentions, or the elements of their state of mind and the history which put them in this position. Time and again, the defendants sought to defend their actions to the judges. The judges rejected such evidence. Even to the very last of the Clayoquot trials, the defendants persisted in attempting to bring in their concerns about clearcut logging as evidence of their intent. But such evidence entered a legal vacuum. The clearcutting of ancient forests is of international concern. Yet the judges kept posing their two questions: Were you there? Did you hear the injunction read? If the answer was "yes," then the defendant was guilty.

The only time the Clayoquot defendants were allowed to introduce a statement which indicated they had gone to stop the clearcutting, not to insult the courts, was after the judge had found them guilty and they were invited to "speak to sentence." At sentencing (which of course comes at the end of a trial after the judge has given a guilty verdict), defendants have the opportunity to give the judge information about their personal situation, information that allows the judge to tailor the punishment so as to take the situation of the defendant into consideration. It was at this point that many of the Clayoquot supporters took the opportunity to explain that they had gone to the bridge to stop the clearcutting.

By the time of the pronouncement of sentence, however, the trial is virtually over, the defendant found guilty. The judges listened to the sentence statements but their boredom was often evident. Yet not everyone was bored, these statements to sentence often brought tears to the eyes of the other members of the court, such as court reporters, court clerks and spectators. The Clayoquot statements should really be gathered and published, for they give a superb account of the present mental state of many citizens who are seeing the destruction of our Earth.

Naturally enough, some of the Clayoquot supporters used their statements at the time of sentencing to tell the judges honestly that they thought they had been treated unfairly. They did so, because they believed sincerely that judges needed to know this. Unfortunately, this honesty was sometimes treated as further contempt of court. Carol Johnson, a professor from the University of Victoria, received a much harsher sentence than the others in her group as a result of her forthright address. She also received a stern lecture from the judge for what he termed her intellectual arrogance.[32] In my own case, the judge clearly did not like what I had to say. He wanted contrition. Such an attitude misses the point of civil disobedience.

In all the many strange twists taken by the Clayoquot trials, the refusal on the part of the judges to listen to the defendants' "justification" signalled that there was something seriously amiss with the trial procedure and the whole conception of criminal contempt. Both inside and outside the courtroom, many observers concluded that the judges were using the law to muzzle the citizenry and to assist the corporate sector. In all discussions of morality, what remains central is the intention with which the action is undertaken. Immanuel Kant, for instance, pointed out that an action that benefited the community could not be called morally good if the action were undertaken for bad reasons. To be "moral" according to Kant, the action must be undertaken for moral reasons. Certainly in criminal cases, under the Criminal Code, the defendant's intentions count for a great deal, as is only natural. Yet because the Clayoquot trials were about criminal contempt of a court injunction, the defendant's intentions went for nought. That no evidence could be introduced from the defendants, meant that the trial was actually a form of show trial. Protestors were already guilty before the trial began. As an onlooker commented after one of the trials: "They didn't need to give you a trial. They could've given you a ticket at the Bridge—'Go to Jail.'" Basically that is what happened, but each of the trials took about three weeks.

* * *

To show what could have been achieved in the trials if the Clayoquot supporters had been allowed to present evidence of their intentions, let us turn briefly to look at the one trial that proved an exception. In this trial the defendants were permitted to submit evidence on their own behalf. At the end, they were still found guilty, but at least they had the satisfaction of knowing that they had been given a real trial. The trial in question was the one involving the group of international Greenpeace activists, which took place in March 1994. The interesting feature in this trial was that the lawyers, Glen Orris and Ken Westlake, did an end-run around the criminal contempt issue. Instead of talking about criminal contempt, they made a challenge on the basis of the

Canadian Charter of Rights and argued that the logging in Clayoquot denied the protestors one of their essential rights under the Charter, that is the right to life and security of life. Judge Hall (ironically the judge who had extended the latest injunction) allowed the challenge on the basis of the Charter to go ahead, and as a result the Clayoquot supporters were able to present, for the first time, an expert witness to testify as to the dangers of clearcutting.

The witness was Dr. Elliot Norse, the scientist who had coined the term bio-diversity. His evidence about the dangers to the west coast forests and fisheries, to the planet itself, was enormously compelling.[33] For once, Crown Counsel had nothing to say. In addition, because of the nature of the case—the Charter challenge—the defendants themselves were allowed to describe their own intentions in going to the bridge, their fears for the planet. This is not the place to rehearse the testimony of the trial. My point is that for the first time it looked as though the central issues were being discussed. It looked as though we had a trial that was a real trial. Although the evidence given by Dr. Norse and the defendants seemed overwhelming to the observers, and certainly the Crown Counsel had little to offer in rebuttal, the judge in the end once again ruled against the defendants. For Judge Hall, it seemed enough that the planet had survived from the time of Marcus Aurelius. He didn't see why clearcutting the Clayoquot would interfere with anyone's right to life.

The other interesting thing in the case of the international group centred on their sentence. How would the judge sentence this group of internationally known and respected senior members of Greenpeace Germany, Austria, the Netherlands, the United Kingdom and the United States, as well as three Canadians? It should be pointed out that the international group had gone much further than most of the earlier protestors. They chained their arms inside concrete blocks that were painted to look like stumps, and it took the police most of the day to release them. In addition, they made their protest late in the autumn after Mr. Justice Bouck had made his ruling in the first trial.

Clearly they were the group who had most flagrantly and openly defied the court order. Everyone feared they would receive long sentences and waited with baited breath to hear Mr. Justice Hall's ruling. When the sentence was pronounced, there was a gasp of amazement—no jail sentence! A fine of $500.00—one of the lightest sentences of the mass trials. Was Judge Hall so moved by the testimony that he gave the defendants a seemingly light sentence? Or did he not want to imprison high-profile international figures and so cause an international scandal? Or perhaps even bring more attention to MacMillan Bloedel's commercial interests. Would there be even a greater backlash against MacMillan Bloedel if the international offenders were jailed?

\* \* \*

Having raised the issue of the sentencing in the case of the international group, this is perhaps a good place to consider the sentencing in general. The sentences differed significantly one from another. Some people received sentences of 45 days and fines of $1500.00; others received sentences of seven days with no fines.[34] Some people were given lengthy probation periods, others none. Some sentences were suspended. Community service was interpreted in widely differing ways and the hours given to different people varied enormously. Some of the judges claimed that these differing sentences guaranteed that the Clayoquot people were receiving individual treatment. This rationalization flies in the face of a basic legal axiom: that similar "crimes" should be punished with similar sentences. Clearly, the judges in the Clayoquot trials had their own ideas of the seriousness of the charge. In the end, the sentences themselves became a scandal.

The most obvious case of extreme sentences occurred with the first trial presided over by Mr. Justice Bouck. Everyone was found guilty, the general sentence being 45 days with fines of from $1,000 to $3,000.[35] The severity of the sentences—serious jail time for a first offence—captured the public's attention right across Canada. Many political cartoons were generated showing hardened criminals and non-violent Clayoquot protestors ending up in the same cell. One of the convicted Clayoquot protestors tells of going to Willingdon Prison where he met a young man convicted of car theft. When they exchanged comments on their situations, the car thief laughed at the sentences handed out to the Clayoquot people, and joked: "This is my third time and I'm getting less time than you." "Yes," came the reply, "but you didn't steal a car from MacMillan Bloedel. Try that next time, and see what you get."

At the time, columnist Jim Gibson wrote in the *Victoria Times-Colonist* of his misgivings about the severity of the Clayoquot sentences.[36] He discussed a recent trial concerning a person who had deliberately run his car into a cyclist. Gibson compared the 45 days given to Clayoquot protestors for sitting on the road with the $100.00 fine given to a person who had deliberately run into a cyclist with his car. Was this justice? Fortunately, when those from the first trial appealed Mr. Justice Bouck's severe sentences, the Appeal Court dismissed the fines, but the 45 day sentences remained.

Moreover, once Mr. Justice Bouck had set the precedent, it became difficult for his brother judges in later trials to alter it, although they did decrease the jail sentence. In fairness, some of the judges in later trials were unhappy with the earlier sentences, and with the trial situation itself. But the judiciary must show solidarity. And to make sure it did, there was at least one occasion on which the Chief Justice slipped into a seat in the backrow of the courtroom to make sure that his judges kept the pressure on. Despite this obvious pressure, many of the later judges worked hard to lighten the sentences, making it possible for people to have electronic monitoring, instead of a jail sentence. Still, even with more realistic judges, the jail sentences seemed way out of line.

Across Canada one could hear the derisive laughter. According to the eastern newspapers, loony B.C. was at it again—imprisoning its citizens for daring to stand up to its government and a corporate giant. And why "loony"? One has only to look at how

Ontario had handled the recent Temagami protests against the destruction of the last stand of white pine to see how a sensible judiciary operates. Because Ontario courts had dispensed with the use of injunctions, the protestors all received individual trials, with legal counsel, and the citizens were not pitted against their own provincial government. The Temagami protest was not seen as defiance of the rule of law, but as a people protesting a logging decision. In fact, throughout the rest of Canada, the courts have abolished the use of court injunctions in public protests, seeing it as a legal barbarism. Out in B.C., however, the courts were still using law by decree, as they had in their earliest days when the province was a colony, when they had dispensed "frontier justice" with a company or corporate tilt. Clayton Ruby, an eminent criminal lawyer from Ontario, stated at a Clayoquot forum: "The law will never change until it stops protecting the interests of big business."[37]

While the severity of the sentences created an uproar with the public, and the protestors were clearly unhappy, the point in the trials that probably caused most concern to the Clayoquot supporters was the tenor of Mr. Justice Bouck's remarks during the trial. Bouck described what had happened at Clayoquot as an "illegal public tantrum."[38] He repeatedly commented that the environmentalists were undermining democracy. As he said: "...contempt proceedings are taken primarily to preserve the rule of law. Without the rule of law democracy will collapse...The strongest mob will rule over the weak. Anarchy will prevail."[39] In Mr. Justice Bouck's eyes the peaceful protests at Kennedy River Bridge were equated with mob rule. His remarks were peppered with comments about armed struggle, with MacMillan Bloedel coming out the victor. He seemed to have convinced himself that the Peace Camp was the Red Brigade, that the Clayoquot supporters were being tried for treason. To Mr. Justice Bouck, peaceful civil disobedience threatened to overthrow Western civilization.

Moreover, these comments were picked up by subsequent judges and repeated. At the next trial, Mr. Justice Low told the Clayoquot defendants before him that he would not tolerate

"Bouck's louts" in his courtroom. Clearly this was an attack on the accuseds' credibility. If they were "louts," then the learned trial judge did not have to listen to their evidence, since louts could not be treated as credible witnesses.

In the early trials, one felt that the judges were frightened for their lives—so cut off from the public did they appear to be. How, one wondered, could our judiciary become so separated from what was actually happening in the province? In what sort of world did they live? My own judge, in one of the final trials, explained at some length how our actions were a danger to the state. I can still recall how, when he made this comment, we all turned to one another with disbelief. Indeed, this paranoid attitude on the part of the judges has brought the courts into more contempt than anything the protestors themselves could have done.

What the judges assumed time and again was that because there were so many protestors at Kennedy River Bridge, they must have constituted a mob. Moreover, they argued that even if the Clayoquot people had not engaged in violence, they were causing the loggers to resort to violence. In any case, the judges convinced themselves that violence was, or could be, involved, and that therefore the defendants in front of them should be sentenced severely. Yet in any act of civil disobedience, the very nature of the act is that it remain peaceful. Persons engaging in civil disobedience break a minor law, but do so, as Martin Luther King said, with love for the law. As has been seen, the idea is that they commit a minor infraction, in order to bring attention to a much greater injustice. The assumption is that society will then cause the government to take a second look at the situation and possibly change it. The conclusion that one draws from the judges' extraordinary reactions to the peaceful protests was that they were either completely out of touch with other citizens or that they were purposefully misinterpreting what happened at the Peace Camp in order to have an excuse to protect the logging companies. I don't know which conclusion is worse.

\* \* \*

It will be worth pausing for a moment here to discuss a point of view that one sometimes hears about the Clayoquot sentences. This is that, since the defendants knowingly engaged in civil disobedience, they should simply "take their lumps" in the courts. The President of the B.C. Civil Liberties Association argued that "protesters must accept the penalties with equanimity, knowing that it is the law, not them, that is wrong."[40] On the surface, this may seem like a fair comment. Why then did so many of the Clayoquot supporters not plead guilty and accept punishment? The answer is simple: they did not believe they were guilty of *criminal contempt*. When one pleads guilty, it is normally because one believes that one is guilty, and none of the protestors I talked to believed that they had travelled to Kennedy River Bridge in order to insult the court.

For various reasons, some of the protestors did plead guilty to criminal contempt. Among these people were those that had to return to work immediately and could not afford three weeks away from their jobs. Others pleaded guilty because they believed that the courts were irrelevant to the real issue. For them, the crucial point was to save the old-growth forests, and that was not happening in the courtroom. These people believed that it made sense to plead guilty in the hopes of obtaining a lighter sentence so that they could then return to the real job of saving the trees. For example, Maurice and Margot Gibbons (contributors to this volume) saw early on that there was no way that they could win against the charge of criminal contempt. They consulted with lawyers and came away persuaded that they would be wasting time and money to put themselves into the meat grinder of the Clayoquot trials. They pleaded guilty but emphasized that they felt no remorse for what they had done. Like many others, they also believed that the courts had put themselves in the position of being at best irrelevant to, and at worst an obstacle to the important issues facing the planet today.

What about the other Clayoquot supporters? Some admitted to

the basic facts of their being at the bridge and hearing the court order read. Some admitted civil contempt but not criminal contempt. For these people, the idea was to save the court time. Such people wanted to argue substantive issues. What they realized too late was that the court did not permit the arguing of substantive issues. (My fellow contributor, Loÿs Maingon, for example, developed a weighty argument, framed in case law, and building upon the environmental evidence of Dr. Gordon Brent Ingram, but the judge disallowed it all. Indeed, the idea for this series of essays arose from the fact that none of this evidence was allowed.)

In short, the answer to why people refused to admit guilt was that they did not believe that they were guilty of criminal contempt. They could not, in conscience, plead guilty to an offence they did not believe they had committed. The problem lay with the "charge" of criminal contempt itself, and by forcing it upon the Clayoquot defendants, the courts caused themselves an enormous amount of wasted time, energy and extra costs.

This matter of the costs of the trials came up frequently. In fact, at one point there was a move to make the defendants pay for the costs through high fines. And yet it was not the defendants who prolonged the proceedings, but the courts themselves through their "charge" of criminal contempt. On the proposal to make the Clayoquot accused pay for the court costs, Peter Scott commented, "Perhaps [the Crown] would ask Christ to pay for his cross, and Joan of Arc to pay for her firewood."[41] It is a sorry state of affairs when one has to be wealthy to protest.

\* \* \*

Having discussed the manner in which the "charge" of criminal contempt itself created problems, I wish now to raise an even thornier question: Were the trials politically motivated or manipulated? This was an accusation made frequently in the newspapers and talk shows after the first severe sentences were handed down. The fact that the government purchased its 50 million dollars worth of MacMillan Bloedel shares shortly before announcing the Clayoquot compromise of April 13th sparked those suspicions. As a major shareholder in MacMillan Bloedel, the government obviously had an interest in squelching the protests. If the protests succeeded in stopping the clearcutting, then MacMillan Bloedel would lose a portion of valuable old-growth trees and its profits would be driven down.[42] The government knew also that the blockades, with all their attendant publicity about the poor logging practices, were giving MacMillan Bloedel a bad name in other countries, and there was a danger that these countries would stop buying MacMillan Bloedel products (as in fact has occurred). Moreover, because of the mysterious manner in which contempt had been made criminal instead of civil, many people claimed that this was the government's doing.

Yet all of this was mere speculation at the time. Was it really possible that the courts were not acting independently? Who made the decisions? Was Cabinet somehow involved?

Certainly a large part of the public thought so. Citizens were writing and calling their M.L.A.s and telling them that 45 days in jail was an outlandish sentence for sitting peacefully on a logging road.[43] Newspapers began to talk about the NDP losing the next election over their mishandling of the Clayoquot. In effect, the public outcry over the Clayoquot trials became so loud and sustained that on October 18, 1993, five members of the government, four of them senior Cabinet Ministers, decided that they would squelch the accusations. To this end, Robin Blencoe, Gretchen Brewin, Elizabeth Cull, Andrew Petter and Moe Sihota wrote a public letter to their Vancouver Island constituents in which they sympathized with their constituents' concern about the long jail sentences, but claimed that the government had nothing to do with them. The government, they stated, had not asked for these sorts of trials. The courts were to blame. The Premier of the province, Mike Harcourt, said that he had seen the letter and given it his approval.[44]

In making the claim that the government was not involved, the five were making the distinction between the legislative and judicial branches of government. To quote from their letter:

Over the past few days, many of our constituents have expressed their frustration and anger regarding the conduct of the contempt trial involving Clayoquot protesters and the imposition of prison sentences.... The extent of public anxiety in our communities has caused us great concern.... We are particularly troubled by suggestions that the conduct of the trial and the resulting jail sentences were directed by the premier or the attorney-general.... Put simply, it was *the courts that commenced and conducted action against the Clayoquot protesters,* not the government" (my emphasis).[45]

From the very start, this letter is misleading, for it omits to mention that Cabinet had decided to allow MacMillan Bloedel to log in the Clayoquot, and it was this decision that formed the basis for the injunctions. Once the injunctions were permitted, the charges for criminal contempt followed like clockwork. The Cabinet was not directly responsible for the harsh sentences, but then ministers never are. While the government may not have made an affirmative decision to handle the protests by injunction and criminal contempt, it was inevitable that this would happen. Moreover, the government knew this when it gave MacMillan Bloedel its cutting rights.

Although the letter was seen as evasive, it calmed the troubled waters for a few days, but then a very curious event occurred. The Chief Justice of the B.C. Supreme Court, William Esson, climbed onto his bench in order to contradict the five M.L.A.s. Chief Justice Esson took the unusual step of giving his view of how the trials were set in motion. He explained that "the proceedings for contempt launched in July were begun and have been conducted by counsel from the Ministry of the Attorney General."[46] After this statement, the Premier stepped forward and said that nothing more should be said on the matter. The Chief Justice had spoken.[47]

At the time, the newspapers generally concluded that the M.L.A.s had been wrong. As might be expected, many of the columnists had a field day with the politicians and their supposed error. But if one pauses for a moment, it becomes evident that there is something odd here. Two of the five M.L.A.s who wrote the letter, Moe Sihota and Andrew Petter, are lawyers. In fact,

Petter has taught law at the University of Victoria. How could a Professor of Law and another astute lawyer make such an elementary error? After all, one of the first things one learns as a law student is the role of the Attorney General. Moreover, Chief Justice Esson had stated clearly that in these prosecutions, the Attorney General did not act as a member of cabinet: "The Attorney General does not act as a member of government, but as an independent officer of the Crown responsible for maintaining the integrity of the court."[48] Surely it would have been enough for the five to mention this fact about the Attorney General's dual role, and that would have been sufficient to distance the cabinet from the courts. Why did they not do so?

One conclusion is that the Attorney General in British Columbia politics does not always do what he is supposed to do, that there is a great deal more overlap between the Attorney General's actions as a member of cabinet and his actions as an independent officer of the Crown.[49] Certainly the Cabinet takes a lively interest in politically sensitive issues before the courts, as one can tell from their comments. When five members of government try to cover up the person or office responsible for criminalizing the contempt proceedings, then it leaves the impression that they want to protect the government from its involvement.

While this speculation about government involvement in the court procedures is interesting in itself, it also returns us to the question asked by the Clayoquot supporters all through the trials: Who was the person responsible for bringing the charge of criminal contempt? Chief Justice Esson had seemed to clarify the point when he said that it was "counsel from the Ministry of the Attorney General." Yet there is something bothersome here, something that does not fit. In his explanation, Chief Justice Esson had also given a little of the history of criminal contempt in B.C., and he noted that no one converted the contempt from civil to criminal. To support his point, he quoted Mr. Justice Wood in the Everywoman's case: "That from the moment the defendants acted in this case, the contempt was a criminal contempt."[50] But if this is the case, then it means that the offence of blockading the Kennedy River Bridge had always been criminal contempt.

It would appear then that the five M.L.A.s were not so wrong after all. If the judge knew that the actions had *always* been criminal contempt, then it was the judge who had decided it was criminal contempt. The judge might then tell, invite, or induce the Attorney General's office to prosecute, but in a very real sense it is the court who initiates contempt proceedings. This point was in fact confirmed when Lloyd MacKenzie, a retired Supreme Court Judge and the newly appointed Information Officer of the Supreme Court, was questioned by reporters and conceded that "it is the judge, after reviewing all the evidence, who decides if the conduct of the protestors is civil or criminal contempt."[51] That the court was involved from the beginning can also be seen in the way that "MacMillan Bloedel vs the Clayoquot supporters" was never changed to "the Crown vs the Clayoquot supporters." This is the way it should have happened, but because it did not, Sihota and Petter concluded quite correctly that the courts, not the Attorney General, had set the whole process going. And one can understand why. The Clayoquot supporters had not broken a law of the land; they had broken a court injunction made by a judge. And the judges were resentful.

* * *

To this point, the discussion of possible political manipulation has been viewed largely in the context of the "charge" of criminal contempt. But there is also the possibility of an even more subtle manipulation, and this last point takes us to the crux of the trials. If one steps back for a moment, one can ask the question: *Should the courts have granted MacMillan Bloedel the court injunction in the first place?* This point was touched on briefly earlier, but I would now like to examine it in more detail. Mostly what people know about injunctions (the exact legal term is a court order or court injunction) comes from what they hear from marital disputes and the like. In the case of a violent marital dispute, a judge will often grant an order restraining the abusive spouse from contact with his partner. In such cases, orders are valuable. But when injunctions/orders are given in situations where citizens are claiming that a company should not be given the right to clearcut public old-growth forests, we have moved to a different situation altogether.[52]

In normal injunctions, the court names certain people and enjoins them not to do particular named acts. In the Clayoquot situation, MacMillan Bloedel had gone to the courts and obtained an injunction against certain named protestors. But later when the company could not name all the people at the protest, the court extended the injunction so that it named the earlier protestors but also "John Doe and Jane Doe and persons unknown." In other words, it was now MacMillan Bloedel against the world. Such wide-ranging latitude is always open to abuse.

David Martin, a Vancouver lawyer, has argued that the granting of the injunction in the first place was an extremely poor way to proceed.[53] As he has noted, it was always open to the police to lay charges against those who wanted to protect the forests. The police had many choices available, such as mischief and trespass. Such charges are under the Criminal Code, and would generally be of a summary nature. There was no need for an injunction.

A second reason why the injunctions were inappropriate in the Clayoquot situation can be seen if one stops to consider the sort of situation that allows for an injunction. As has been noted, injunctions follow the commencement of a civil suit. In the Clayoquot situation, MacMillan Bloedel had begun a civil suit some years earlier (Sept. 16, 1991) against Sheila Simpson and others, and then applied for an injunction (Sept. 18, 1991) so that they could proceed with work while the case was getting underway. But over the years there was no evidence that MacMillan Bloedel was pursuing its civil case, although Mr. Justice Tysoe urged them to do so. The company was using the injunction as a means of avoiding the difficulties of a civil trial, a trial in which it would have had to defend its logging practices. Hence, for the courts to extend and re-extend the original injunction meant that they were aiding MacMillan Bloedel to circumvent the appropriate legal process. Since there has to be a mechanism to enforce the injunction (the jail sentences), the courts were also putting the force of the state behind the efforts of MacMillan Bloedel to advance its own interests. In effect, the courts were creating a private criminal law for MacMillan Bloedel. No wonder that the supporters of Clayoquot concluded that the courts were "in bed" with MacMillan Bloedel. Not only that, but the use of an injunction creates a situation which pits the judiciary against its citizens instead of the Plaintiff and the Defendant.

Another way of looking at these injunctions in cases where the public takes to the streets to protest a social issue, is to note how the judge's injunction removes the ability of the Attorney General to pursue the case under the Criminal Code. In other words, through its use of injunctions, the court usurps the right of the Attorney General to enforce existing laws. In so doing, the court makes its own law, but it does so without any of the safeguards of normal criminal law. As was seen, the procedures for dealing with criminal contempt are a quagmire of uncertainties, and leave the defendant with no real defence.

The use of injunctions in cases of public protest are dangerous for several other reasons as well. As the Clayoquot supporters discovered, injunctions such as the one granted to MacMillan Bloedel are given *ex parte*, which means that only one party has to appear before the judge. In other words, MacMillan Bloedel applied to a judge and was granted the injunction without anyone "from the other side" being there to question the need for the injunction. Now there is no doubt that MacMillan Bloedel had the "legal" right to be logging in Clayoquot. They held Tree Farm Licence 44, a lease that gives them cutting rights on public land. But they had also been found numerous times to be in violation of fisheries regulations, having damaged important salmon streams. When an injunction is given, the person or company receiving the injunction is supposed to come with "clean hands." Could MacMillan Bloedel claim to have clean hands when its logging practices had been in violation numerous times? Writing in

*The Vancouver Sun*, Stephen Hume noted that he was "not aware of a single forest company president being required to take executive responsibility" for the massive damage to salmon-bearing streams, and yet the courts were quick to make "civil disobedience a criminal act."[54]

If injunctions against public acts of protest are so dangerous, how is it that the British Columbia courts still hand them out so easily? It is interesting to reflect for a moment that the use of injunctions arose in the context of labour disputes and proved a very convenient method for the government to intervene on the side of the employers. In earlier days, labour tended to be seen by the government as a problem. Courts handed out injunctions in order to curb the power of labour, especially the power of the unions, in situations where the companies needed the help of the courts and the government. This point was made cogently by two B.C. judges recently (McEachern and Southin) while commenting on the contempt convictions associated with the Everywoman's Health Centre: "By the 1950's, the courts of British Columbia were thought by some to be anti-labour because of the number of injunctions granted in labour disputes."[55] In the Clayoquot case, the fact that the court was willing to give an injunction to a logging company against the public, just as earlier they had given them against the unions, made it seem as though the courts still saw their role as the protector of the property rights of those with great wealth.

For anyone following this argument closely, the mention of the role of injunctions in curbing unions should sound familiar. Let us return for a moment to the case mentioned earlier, that of the Alberta Nurses. The Alberta Nurses *Union*. As was seen, Madam Justice McLachlin upheld the charge of criminal contempt—in the case against the Union. It was her decision that formed the precedent for the Clayoquot trials. In other words, the Clayoquot was being seen through the lens of a labour dispute.

To put the matter even more sharply into focus, we can now look at the Alberta Nurses case from the point of view of some of the dissenting opinions from Supreme Court Justices sitting on the case. While dissenting opinions are not binding on later judges, they often make the more interesting reading. Justice Cory (and the lawyers at our trials indicated that Cory's was the real legal mind to watch for informed opinion) attempted to open up the whole issue of public protest and to see it in a larger social arena. He argued that "the use of criminal contempt proceedings and such crushing penalties is inappropriate except in circumstances of violence or threats of serious violence."[56] Clearly the Clayoquot protest did not fall into this category, since it was peaceful.

Cory also argued that "Intentional defiance of a court order, which takes place in full public view, may well be a significant factor in leading a court to conclude that there had been an injury to the public interest. However, to make it the sole determining factor extends the scope of criminal contempt powers far beyond the limits necessary to achieve their end."[57] Cory was clearly aware of the dangers of the court using injunctions to silence dissent of any sort. He said that if the courts continued to rely on injunctions in such cases then "the courts will no longer be seen as impartial arbiters but as society's instruments for imposing crushing penalties on unions." Not just on unions, one might add, but on any group of citizens that press for change.

One last comment from Cory. He notes that "Unions sometimes have no alternative but to take strike action and by means of peaceful picketing put forward their position to the public. If publicity is chosen as the element which transforms civil into criminal contempt, then it will often deny the public access to the union's position."[58] When one compares Cory's comments to those of McLachlin, one can see that Cory has a far greater sense of the role of the law in social disputes. Unfortunately, McLachlin's position has prevailed in the courts, although she may well alter her opinions once she sees how her views have been used in British Columbia.

Having spoken of manipulation, I wish now to suggest another sort of manipulation within the court system. This involved the choice of judges to preside over the cases. There are in fact over

100 Supreme Court judges available, but the Clayoquot trials were tried, not by the younger and more liberal judges, but mainly by the older and more conservative ones. Moreover, once one asks about the background of these judges, one discovers that they generally worked as lawyers for law firms who did a great deal of work for large companies, and in B.C., that inevitably means the large logging companies and the resource industries. Moreover, throughout the trial, there was never any provision to require full disclosure of the judges. To ask a judge to declare that he had no shares in MacMillan Bloedel, and thus was not a party to the case, is reason in itself for further contempt.

Having discussed some of the ways in which the court favoured the large corporations, I now want to examine similar favouritism within the RCMP. The first point to note is that the RCMP is under contract to the provincial government (who, as was seen, is a large shareholder in MacMillan Bloedel). Throughout the Clayoquot summer of 1993, the RCMP had a special detachment at Ucluelet to deal with the ongoing protests at the Kennedy River Bridge. To give the force credit, they performed their role at the Bridge reasonably well. In the daily arrests, they generally behaved with exemplary even-handedness to the protestors. Especially in front of the cameras, the RCMP treated them civilly. Some of the protestors even wrote letters to the RCMP, thanking the special detachment for their courtesy.

There was, however, another side to the RCMP activities that occurred when the cameras were not operating. Many of the Clayoquot supporters employed passive resistance—they went limp when arrested—and this meant that, after an arrest, the RCMP officers had to carry them to the police vehicles. So long as the cameras were rolling, the police were willing to carry the protestors, but once out of sight of the cameras the RCMP decided that they could stop playing what they saw as a "game," and they demanded that the protestors walk. If the protestors continued to take their peaceful civil disobedience seriously, they were treated roughly. On the day of my own arrest, the crowd of bystanders had to call for the cameras to ensure that the arrestees were treated fairly.

Much more serious from a political point of view is the evidence that the RCMP actively collaborated with MacMillan Bloedel. Throughout the Clayoquot summer of 1993, the Peace Camp made every attempt to keep the RCMP officers informed of upcoming activities. The philosophy of the Peace Camp was that the protest should be entirely peaceful and that no animosity should be shown, even to those who favoured clearcutting the Clayoquot. As a result the Peace Camp developed a close working relation with the RCMP, keeping them informed of the approximate numbers of people to be arrested. Clearly this cooperation made the RCMP's job much easier.

Even without such close cooperation from the Peace Camp, the RCMP had an obligation to protect, not only MacMillan Bloedel, but also the Clayoquot supporters. Given the helpfulness of those in the Peace Camp towards the RCMP, one would have thought that human nature would have led the RCMP to be especially vigilant for the interests of the Camp. If anything, it worked the other way. On at least two occasions after a protest at the Bridge (July 15th and November 9th), the Clayoquot supporters found that the loggers and SHARE people (an organization funded by the Forest Alliance to promote the companies' interests) had blockaded the road to the Peace Camp, so as to prevent their leaving. When the people from the Peace Camp asked for help from the RCMP officer to clear the road and let them pass, he replied that he would. In both cases, he then drove up to the barricade, talked to the SHARE people, and then drove on through, waving back at those from the Peace Camp and leaving them in a potentially dangerous situation.

One could add a long list of such incidents of bias,[59] but I want to turn now to a much larger incident, one that has, in the view of many people, permanently damaged the reputation of the Force. I am referring to the fact that the RCMP gave their evidence to MacMillan Bloedel in return for evidence that MacMillan Bloedel collected. When the news media first released information that such collusion was taking place between the

RCMP and MacMillan Bloedel, a shock wave went through the population. In the beginning, most people assumed that the exchange had taken place only once, and that it was an accident. Some junior constable, I imagined, had been overzealous. Then it came out that the RCMP had been meeting with MacMillan Bloedel employees on a daily basis, at Smiley's Cafe, over the entire summer to exchange evidence. Even as I write this now, it strikes me as incredible that this took place. The RCMP supplied MacMillan Bloedel with the RCMP "mug shots" taken of each arrestee, along with personal information: name, address, age, and other details. The MacMillan Bloedel employee gave the RCMP copies of the video taken of that day's protest and any still photos that had been made from the video. Only towards the end of the protests did the RCMP finally become concerned about this practice. As Lawyer Kevin McCullough stated bluntly: "Staff Sergeant Doyle finally pulled the plug on the operation."[60]

During the trials, the two senior officers, Staff Sergeants Johnston and Doyle, were asked many times about this collusion between the RCMP and MacMillan Bloedel. And one finds many different answers in the transcripts. In my own trial, Staff Sergeant Johnston said that he could not remember who first instituted the exchange. In later questioning, he mentioned two junior constables. In an earlier trial, he said that he had himself begun the exchange. When asked for his opinion about the exchange, he replied: "...a corporation has access to public record in many spots when people are arrested and taken to court and charged, so it's not like it was a big secret...it was quite alright, appropriate."[61] He also said that he "felt comfortable with the exchange."[62] When Staff Sergeant Doyle was asked why the RCMP exchanged information, he replied: "I can't answer why we did that...it was information they needed...." For *what?*—one wants to ask. When questioned if such exchanges were general practice, Staff Sergeant Doyle answered: "...it was a first time for me."[63] So far as I can learn, there has been no disciplinary action instituted against any of the RCMP officers, and in fact the Force has shown no interest in investigating the situation.

The information that MacMillan Bloedel obtained from this exchange with the RCMP was obviously advantageous to the company, since it gave them identifications of the Clayoquot supporters that they had recorded on their video films. In fact, MacMillan Bloedel created a book of all people arrested, with photographs as well as personal information, including a history of their other environmental activities, and in some cases their Social Insurance Numbers. As one of the lawyers pointed out, the information has now been entered in a data base, which MacMillan Bloedel has made available to other forestry companies. It is of great concern to the people involved that this information has been disseminated in order to prejudice them in future.

In all this, one wonders what the RCMP gained by having the MacMillan Bloedel videos. Nothing very much. The advantage was all on MacMillan Bloedel's side. Here was a case in which citizens were fighting a major company, only to find that their own RCMP was working with the company against them. Ria Bos, a Clayoquot supporter, put it in perspective when she observed: "After the Stanley Cup riots in Vancouver, the CBC refused to give up its videos of the event, claiming that to do so would make them an arm of the police. Did not the exchange of photos between MacMillan Bloedel and the RCMP make the RCMP an arm of MacMillan Bloedel?"

Throughout the Clayoquot summer of 1993, it was often difficult to distinguish between the functions of the employees of MacMillan Bloedel and the RCMP. In a normal case, it is the police who collect the evidence. But in the Clayoquot trials, the individual who did the video filming, the major piece of evidence used in the trials, was a MacMillan Bloedel employee. To give some idea of the implications here, suppose that you are involved in a case where your neighbour complains about you. And the police allow the neighbour to collect all the evidence. What sort of a case will you have? The police, of course, are supposed to collect the evidence. That is what we pay them for. But in the Clayoquot trials, the police felt comfortable allowing MacMillan Bloedel to collect evidence, and the court found no problem in using

MacMillan Bloedel evidence against the Clayoquot supporters.

The manner in which the court, the police and the corporation became virtually indistinguishable in these cases should by now be apparent, and it may be unnecessary to add yet another example. Yet there is one other case that should be looked at briefly, because it shows so unquestionably the systemic relation between the corporation and the institutions of the law. This is the trial of Tzeporah Berman, a young woman who often acted as a spokesperson at the Peace Camp (and one of the contributors to this volume). Her arrest was most unusual and took everyone by surprise. Virtually all the people who were arrested chose to be arrested. It was clearly understood that if you were on the road (and the police actually spray-painted lines along the edge of the road) after the injunction was read, then you could be arrested. Berman, however, was arrested from the side of the road. Early in the summer, she had decided that she could be of most help in the Peace Camp itself, and she took the decision not to put herself in a position to be arrested. How and why was she arrested?

The first response is to say that the police made a mistake in arresting Berman. Yet such mistakes do not usually occur with high-profile people such as Berman. The background to the case is most revealing. As the days passed in the summer of 1993, it became evident that the blockades were gathering momentum. The arrest of individual protestors was not stemming the protest. More people kept arriving. The obvious solution was to arrest the organizers of the Peace Camp. If the Peace Camp could be closed down, then there was a chance of stopping the protests. In conversations with the RCMP, Berman learned that MacMillan Bloedel had lobbied them for some time to have her arrested. But the RCMP had no reason to arrest her, since she never blockaded the road.

In order to have her and other leading figures arrested, MacMillan Bloedel decided to apply to the court to have the injunction expanded so that it would apply to anyone "aiding and abetting" the demonstrations at Kennedy River Bridge. As was mentioned earlier, one can gain an injunction or a change to an injunction _ex parte_, meaning that only the party requesting the injunction need appear. Quite by accident, however, lawyers interested in the Clayoquot learned about this impending application to have the injunction expanded and were on hand to argue against it.[64] Successfully, as it turned out. In the meantime, however, the RCMP were so convinced that the expansion to the injunction would be granted that they arrested Berman from the side of the road. At the time, they told her that she was being arrested for "aiding and abetting." Clearly, they had been well briefed by MacMillan Bloedel that an application had been made to expand the injunction. As was seen, however, the expansion was not granted. Berman had been arrested illegally.

The obvious thing to do in this situation was to drop the charges. Berman had done nothing wrong. Yet when the request was made for the charges to be dropped, the Attorney General's office refused. Why, one wonders? Was it that she had already spent several days in jail as a result of the false arrest, and the Attorney General's office was worried about the consequences? As June 20, 1994—the date for Berman's trial—drew nearer, a general ground swell of interest in the case developed. Many concerned citizens wrote personally to Colin Gabelmann, the Attorney General, asking him to examine the case and drop the charges. Prominent citizens banded together and contributed money to take out full-page ads in the _Victoria Times-Colonist_. Nothing happened. The trial proceeded.

For an entire week the Crown Counsel presented video evidence of Berman's activities at the Kennedy River Bridge, but never once was she seen violating the injunction. It was clear that an enormous number of hours had been put in, combing through all the MacMillan Bloedel videos to find any possible evidence against Berman. Along with a number of others, Berman had been a leading figure at the Peace Camp; she had in fact supported and helped the protestors. Yet this was not really at issue, since the injunction did not rule out such help. As Mr. Justice Low commented: "You can assume that I will find evidence of aiding and abetting" but that was not the point. The issue, he said, was "whether it was prohibited."[65]

As Crown Counsel Ivanesco came towards the close of his evidence, it was clear that he was in trouble with his prosecution. He had no evidence. Indeed, the trouble was becoming so manifest that on the last day of his evidence, Ivanesco suddenly began to present a completely new argument. Mr. Justice Low became irritated. The case was dissolving in a shambles. But why was the Crown Counsel attempting to mount a new case at the eleventh hour? Looking at the documents the Crown Counsel was handing up to the judge in support of his new argument, Berman's lawyer observed that they carried the fax imprint of Davis & Co., one of the law firms that does legal work for MacMillan Bloedel. As the date on the fax sheets indicated, the material had been faxed to Crown Counsel the night before, and the poor man was attempting to use the material to mount a new argument against Berman. Unsuccessfully.

At this point, Berman's lawyer, David Martin, called upon the judge to declare that there was no evidence to proceed with the trial. After deliberating for a short period, Mr. Justice Low agreed and the case was thrown out. It is important to realize that Berman was not found "not-guilty." The case was entirely thrown out.

Berman's case carries dark undertones for the supposed independence of the Crown in these trials. The faxed sheets from Davis & Co. indicate that the Crown was receiving some very expensive legal aid. For the Clayoquot supporters, these faxed sheets offered proof that the trials had not been fair. When the Crown takes over a trial, the plaintiff (in this case MacMillan Bloedel) is supposed to bow out. Moreover, the Crown takes over the trial on the principle that the situation demands that the State intervene to see that society is protected. But when we have the Crown Counsel working from faxed papers from MacMillan Bloedel's lawyers, then it seems as though the Crown has entered into a partnership with MacMillan Bloedel against the accused— those who struggled to protect Clayoquot Sound.

This situation leads one to revisit the earlier question: why did the Attorney General persist with the case after he received masses of letters from ordinary citizens who could all see that Berman had broken no law? One would assume that he could see this as well. Yes, but when the Attorney General is responsible, through his Crown Counsel, for initiating the procedings, and when the Crown Counsel is in partnership with MacMillan Bloedel, then there is clearly no reason or motive to stay proceedings. On the contrary, there is every reason to push on, since there is so little distinction between the Attorney General's Office and MacMillan Bloedel. Indeed, since the provincial government owns part of MacMillan Bloedel, it is, in a very real sense, MacMillan Bloedel.

* * *

What can we conclude about law and order in the Clayoquot? The police, the judges, both claimed they were "just doing their jobs." The police made the arrests. The courts found everyone guilty. Yet law and order was maintained at great cost to the credibility of both the police and the court system. As should now be apparent, the system of injunctions for dealing with the problems of bad logging practices is hopelessly feudal, an invitation to the corporations to use the courts for the creation of their own private criminal law. The charge of criminal contempt that was employed to respond to the violation of the injunction was also hopelessly inappropriate—another form of anti-labour legislation, which results in a kind of frontier justice to protect the large corporations from the public.

We need to remind ourselves, however, that all is not yet concluded. A number of lawyers have applied to the Supreme Court of Canada to appeal the first of the Clayoquot trials, and the Supreme Court's decision will apply to most of the other Clayoquot supporters convicted in later trials. At this point, we have not yet heard whether leave will be granted to appeal. And of course even if leave is granted, we cannot be sure of the outcome. Judges in the Supreme Court of Canada have their political biases as well. What is certain, however, is that our highest court will look at the conduct of the B.C. courts. In the meantime, citizens need to keep abreast of the issues, they need to inform themselves of how the courts have allowed their orders to create private criminal law for the large corporations, they need to recognize that the courts are themselves playing a part in the ongoing destruction of the ancient rainforest of Clayoquot Sound.

## Notes

1. Those who came to the Kennedy River Bridge over the summer of 1993 owe a large debt to the Friends of Clayoquot Sound, which was founded in 1979 by concerned residents of the Sound to stop clearcutting in their "back yard."

2. See Justice Spencer's "Reasons for Judgement," in the trial beginning September 27, 1993, where he says that "those who are carried away in the zeal for their cause...would do well to review them [the trials] quietly..." (p. 4).

3. The reason for the discrepancy in numbers is that some of those arrested were not brought to trial. After the initial arrest, the police would sometimes decide—because the person was too young or too old, and for a whole host of other reasons—to release them without charging them.

4. The accused protestors from August 9th (some 250 in number) were at the outset directed officially to the Newcombe Auditorium in Victoria for their trial.

5. "An open, flagrant and public defiance of a Court Order" was one of the key phrases used to define criminal contempt. See Madam Justice McLachlin's "Reasons for Judgement," April 16, 1992, in U.N.A. v. Alberta (Attorney General) [S.C.C.], p. 493.

6. See Transcripts of Judge Bouck's trial, beginning August 30, 1993, Vol 1, pp. 55-56.

7. See "Outline of the Crown's Submission on behalf of John Vedova," where Crown states that "the facts surrounding the matter before the Court are not such that Counsel is essential for a fair trial."

8. See "Reasons for Judgement of Chief Justice McEachern" in the Court of Appeal Registry, March 28, 1993. Note as well Justice Lambert's highly interesting dissenting opinion.

9. The Transcripts contain many references to "Unidentified Speaker." Sometimes the unidentified person is clearly a defendant, sometimes not. For example, see Transcript of the Bouck Trial, Volume 1, p. 135.

10. His name has been withheld to protect his reputation.

11. This appeal was undertaken by Peck and Tammen, Orris Burns, Ritchie &

Company, James W. Millar. See their "Amended Factum," pp. 36-45, No. V02011, Victoria Registry.

12. The Transcript for this part of the trial should be compulsory reading for all law students. Transcript, Volume 1, pp. 110-111.

13. My own probation order, signed by Justice Hutchison, states that I was convicted of criminal contempt "under the Criminal Code," when in fact it was under Common Law. Such inaccuracies have caused a number of people serious problems at the border. No one knows exactly how the mistakes affect police records.

14. Both Mr. Justice Hutchison and Madam Justice Saunders speak of the "charge" of criminal contempt in their "Reasons for Judgement." See January 5, 1993, and January 29, 1993.

15. See Madam Justice Saunders in her "Reasons for Judgement," January 29, 1993.

16. Chief Justice Esson in his "Oral Reasons for Judgement," March 18, 1991.

17. See Mr. Justice Drost's "Reasons for Judgement," July 24, 1992, p. 2.

18. See Mr. Justice Gow's "Reasons for Sentencing," Nov. 13, 1992.

19. Mr. Justice MacDonell, in his "Reasons for Judgement" in a trial soon after that presided over by Drost, mentions that "the civil contempt was converted to criminal contempt...by the order of Mr. Justice Drost" (October 30, 1992), p. 1.

20. See the "Proceedings at Sentencing before the Honourable Mr. Justice Gow," Dec. 18, 1992. The case in question does not concern MacMillan Bloedel but Fletcher Challenge.

21. See "Reasons for Judgement of the Honourable Mr. Justice Flood," in the case heard in Victoria on September 23-26, 1991.

22. The terminology is itself confusing, and the judges found difficulty in keeping the terms separate. Criminal contempt was being treated in the civil style of proceeding, not under the Criminal Code, but under Common Law.

23. It appears that the main criterion for whether one appears in CPIC is whether one is fingerprinted. The Clayoquot supporters were not.

24. See Transcript for the first trial, Vol. 1, p. 70.

25. See Mr. Justice Lambert's dissenting opinion in the B.C. Court of Appeal's Decision, Feb. 11, 1994, p. 43.

26. See Transcript of the trial beginning, June 6, 1994.

27. The Court Clerk always called the case as it was written on the Court bulletin boards: MacMillan Bloedel v. Simpson et al. At my own trial, it was only at the "sentencing" that this rubric was changed for the first time to "MacMillan Bloedel v. Ronald B. Hatch."

28. See United Nurses of Alberta v. Alberta (Attorney General) 1992, in *Western*

*Weekly Reports*, 1992, pp. 481-485.

29. Mr. Justice Hutchison, in his "Oral Reasons for Judgement," on October 30, 1991, stated that the difference between criminal and civil contempt "does not lack for authoritative jurisprudence. Indeed, it might be argued to have received more comment than clarity" (p. 4).

30. See *W.W.R.*, 1992, p. 482.

31. See *W.W.R.*, 1992, p. 482.

32. See the *Victoria Times-Colonist*, Nov. 2, 1993, A1.

33. Dr. Norse's testimony is available in the Transcripts for the trial beginning Feb. 10, 1994.

34. The Friends of Clayoquot Sound in Tofino keep a complete record of all the sentences. Frances Bula, writing in *The Vancouver Sun*, lists some of the very serious crimes that merited sentences of 45 days in jail (Oct. 20, 1993, A15).

35. One repeat offender received a jail sentence of 60 days and a fine of $3,000.00.

36. The *Victoria Times-Colonist*, Oct. 20, 1993.

37. Clayton Ruby, in an oral presentation at "Clearcutting Clayoquot: Global Perspectives, Local Concerns," a public forum on Clayoquot at the Robson Square Conference Centre, Vancouver, Feb. 8, 1994.

38. Judge Bouck's "Reasons for Sentencing," Oct. 6-13, p. 9. Repr. in part in the *Globe and Mail*, October 18, 1993.

39. Judge Bouck's "Reasons for Sentencing," Oct. 6-13, p. 5.

40. Andrew Wilkinson, "On Civil Disobedience: the Forest for the Trees," in *The Democratic Commitment*, vol. 27, no. 4, Dec. 1993, pp. 1-2.

41. The *Victoria Times-Colonist*, Oct. 7, 1993, A2.

42. Most of the large logging companies have difficulties selling second-growth timber abroad. Old-growth timber, of the kind found in the Clayoquot, is much more valuable.

43. By Friday, October 15th, a great many people were making allegations that the Attorney General had "himself steered the Clayoquot Sound protestors' case through the courts and called the shots along the way." Various radio show hosts had claimed that either "Gabelmann or the provincial cabinet were instrumental in elevating the charges from civil contempt to the more serious criminal contempt, or were behind the decision to charge the protestors at all." See Keith Baldrey, in *The Vancouver Sun*, Oct. 16, 1993. In a rare interview, Ernie Quantz, the Asst. Deputy Minister for Criminal Justice, stated publicly that Gabelmann "was not involved in the process. There was absolutely no political involvement at all." Gabelmann confused the issue further when he used the "royal we" to state: "Everybody assumes we lay contempt charges, but we don't."

See *The Vancouver Sun*, Oct. 16, 1993.

44. See the *Victoria Times-Colonist*, October 23, 1993, A1 & A2.

45. This letter of October 18, 1993, was sent out to thousands of Vancouver Island constituents; it was then made public and reprinted in part in *The Vancouver Sun*, Nov. 5, 1993, A15.

46. See Chief Justice Esson's statement from the Bench, entitled "Statement re: Contempt Hearings Arising from Injunction in MacMillan Bloedel Limited v. Simpson et al," p. 1. Esson read his statement in court October 22, 1993, and he then released it publicly. It was reprinted in part in *The Vancouver Sun*, Oct. 23, 1993, & Nov. 5, 1993, A15.

47. Harcourt is quoted in Keith Baldrey's article, "Chief Justice flays cabinet ministers," in *The Vancouver Sun*, Oct. 23, 1993.

48. Esson, "Statement," p. 3.

49. The potential overlap of the Attorney General's duties has led commentators to call for an independent prosecutor, separate from the Attorney General. See Gil McKinnon & Keith Hamilton's "Get the politics out of crime; Get a DPP [Director of Public Prosecutions]," in *The Vancouver Sun*, April 26, 1994.

50. Esson, "Statement," p. 8. Ernie Quantz, the Asst. Deputy Minister for Criminal Justice, is quoted as saying that "the Clayoquot Sound protestors found themselves facing criminal contempt largely because of a July 1992 decision by B.C. Supreme Court Judge Ian Drost." See *The Vancouver Sun*, Oct. 16, 1993. This claim became the standard answer by the judiciary and Crown counsel after this point, although Drost nowhere in his Judgement indicates that he expected all further trials to be for criminal contempt. And indeed they were not. Presumably the degree of contempt is something that each judge must find from the circumstances.

51. Reported in *The Vancouver Sun*, Oct. 20, 1993, A3.

52. One of the most sophisticated articles on the dangers of injunctions is that co-authored by Hamar Foster and John McLaren, Professors of Law at the University of Victoria. The article was excerpted in the *Globe and Mail*, Nov. 5, 1993, A19.

53. David Martin, in his newsletter, *Charter of Rights*, Sept. 1993, pp. 1-4. His statements were also reported in *The Vancouver Sun*, Aug. 21, 1993, B10.

54. Stephen Hume, in *The Vancouver Sun*, Sept. 3, 1993.

55. See McEachern and Southin's comment on their judgement in Everywoman's Health Centre v. Bridges Society (1988) (1990), 78 D.L.R (4th) 529, 62 C.C.C. (3d) 455 (C.A.) [*091057060], pp. 541-42. Reprinted in part in David Martin's *Charter of Rights*, September 1993, p.1.

56. See *W.W.R.*, 1992, p. 484.

57. See *W.W.R.*, 1992, p. 484.

58. See *W.W.R.*, 1992, p. 484.

59. Compare the incident when the "white-collar workers" rented a bus and attempted to drive to the bridge on September 1, 1993. For close to three hours, the bus was stopped and boxed-in by loggers and their supporters. The air was let out of the tires, posters ripped off the side of the bus, and the business people verbally assaulted. The RCMP were present throughout, but did nothing. Marty Legg, one of the organizers of the trip, commented: "It's pretty obvious the police were sympathetic to the road blockers." *The Vancouver Sun*, Sept. 2, 1993, A1. There were also a number of incidents when garbage was dumped at the Peace Camp and when rowdies attacked the camp at midnight hours. The RCMP and the Attorney General's office were unwilling to act against those involved. At the camp set up near Victoria in August 1994, hooligans threatened the camp people with blowtorches. The RCMP refused to appear until some U.S. citizens at the camp complained to their Embassy of the threats against their lives.

60. Kevin McCullough, in the trial beginning June 6, 1994.

61. See Transcript for the first trial, Vol. 4, pp. 673 & 686.

62. See Transcript from the trial beginning June 6, 1994.

63. See Transcript for the first trial, Vol 3, pp. 505, 511, 517 & 518.

64. A young law student came across the posted notice while looking for something else. Realizing how important such an expansion of the injunction would be, she literally ran for help. Had she not seen the notice, there would have been no one to oppose the change, and everyone who helped the protest—many tens of thousands of people—would have been at risk.

65. The *Victoria Times-Colonist*, June 24, 1994, B1.

# Clayoquot: Recovering From Cultural Rape

LOŸS MAINGON, PH.D.

*The activities of the mind arise solely from adequate ideas;
the passive states of mind depend solely on inadequate ideas.*
(Spinoza, *Ethica* III, iii, 1665)

In many environmental issues facing us today, including the 1993 protest at Clayoquot Sound, there is a tendency to look only at the immediate issues, such as the clearcutting of ancient forests and the destruction of salmon habitat. Important as these are, it is crucial to look behind immediate issues to their cultural significance. Behind every environmental problem lies a cultural phenomenology. Although the debate over Clayoquot Sound is generally viewed within its political context, the cultural implications are rarely considered, perhaps because culture is now taken for granted. The concept of "culture" refers not only to the arts of so-called "High Culture," but to the broader dynamic web of relations that bind a people together and make social interaction meaningful. Viewed ecologically, a culture is a set of relations whose connectedness produces meaning. A set of relations that destroys or diminishes the sense of connection is not culture, but dysfunctionality. The basis of all functionality is connection to place or environment. Culture arises from connection to and knowledge of places and environments. A meaningful cultural relationship to place is crucial to the production of functional social conditions. Thus, environmental problems are cultural problems because the destruction of the environment is the destruction of culture.

When social unrest arises from abuses of the environment—as in Clayoquot—we can be sure that we are in the midst of a dissenting culture attempting to recover lost social values in order to overcome dysfunctionality. Historically, dissenting groups have always claimed to be seeking to recover cultural structures of meaningfulness. Recognition of the legitimacy of that pursuit involves a recognition of group rights as distinct from societal or individual rights. Clayoquot involves the group rights of environmentalists and the legitimacy of their cultural aspirations.

## Part I:    Cultural Rape

From the environmental movement's point of view, it seems evident that consumer society is dysfunctional. To mainstream society, on the other hand, life seems to go on pretty much as it should. Indeed, the mainstream has difficulty in accepting the significance of what the environmentalists are saying. For students of culture it is a commonplace that, no matter how abnormal a situation may be, it will always seem normal, even comfortable, to those who are immersed in it, so long as they do not stop to question their activity. Thus, rape, infibulation, clitorectomy, infanticide, foot-binding and many other acts of violence that seem unethical to us are perfectly acceptable in other cultures. Ecocide (destruction of our life support system, the earth) which is abhorrent to other cultures, seems to be culturally acceptable in a consumer society. So long as the reality of ecocide can be emotionally deferred, it remains inconceivable to the vast majority of people in modern consumer society who depend on and who place their faith in the power of technology to overcome the natural limits of this world. How is it that consumer society allows ecocide?

Advertising and television have created a passive cynical society which seems to have lost the ability to think critically.[1] As Neil Postman, the American social critic, recently stated:

> For many students, there is something godlike about technology. They are exhilarated when they are in technology's presence. They are depressed and lost when they are denied access to it. They believe that technological innovation is the same thing as human progress.... I tell them they must be critical thinkers and they say: "What is it we must think critically about and for what purpose?"[2]

The awe for technology and the concomitant passive compliance to the status quo are characteristic, not only of Postman's students, but of consumer society at large. This social condition which threatens our humanity and democracy is symptomatic of a loss of connection with the cultural narratives that have ensured human survival on this planet. Technological subservience is a threat to the viability of all the cultural institutions that have enabled our continuity and freedom. A large proportion of the public no longer knows, nor cares, about the origins and meanings of their institutions. Not to recall what made us who we are today leaves us bereft of culture. Democracy is not a prescription of givens; it is a cultural dialogue that depends on participation and criticism. Critical thinking is therefore the cornerstone of democracy. One cannot reflect or think on the significance of cultural institutions such as democracy without a knowledge of our cultural continuity. Culture is the set of tools that enables us to reflect on our identity.[3] The loss of our cultural inheritance to the hegemony of technology is cultural rape.

Cultures are inextricably bound to places which are essential to the psychological health of individuals and social groups.[4] These places sustain meaningful activity and purpose. Cultures are not arbitrary or artificial creations: they are responses to environments that have co-evolved ecologically over the span of human and geographical development. A healthy culture is in touch with its environment, and its responses to it are adapted to maximize survival and diversity.[5]

From a cultural point of view, the Clayoquot Sound debate is

about opposing perceptions of the land and of group cultures re-
acting to the technological homogenization of culture on a global
scale.[6] It is just one instance of growing unrest in response to
global cultural crisis. To understand what the Clayoquot Sound debate means and asks us, we have to come to terms with the basic
conditions under which we know dissenting group cultures. Within
our cultural mindset, the terms of reference used to explain events
serve to adjust these same events to our cultural prejudices. The
facts reported are then not facts, but interpretations that mediate
the facts in order to help us understand the actions of the group
in power.

The struggle for Clayoquot is part of a social phenomenon
known as radical environmentalism, which signals the limits of
technocratic society.[7] Radical environmentalism is a social expression of dissent from the anti-democratic implications of technology. It is heir to the foundations of the liberal democratic
tradition which guarantees the individuality, tolerance and distinctiveness of social groups. The Clayoquot debate is much more
than a question of jobs, loggers and trees—as the media has
made it out to be. Radical environmentalism is a will to recover
the democratic foundations of our cultural heritage which have
been usurped by technocratic pseudo-culture.

## Part II:   The Field and the Map

In each of the forty or more mass trials of the Clayoquot protestors, a key piece of evidence was the map of Clayoquot Sound
presented by the Crown. It was a forestry map of MacMillan
Bloedel's Tree Farm License 44. Simple, passive and apparently
harmless, this map was essential to the Crown's case because it
presented the court with a picture of the geographic relation of
humans to the watersheds in contention. The map formed a
mental picture which would pre-determine the judge's understanding of the various events and places related to the protests,
so that the alleged threat to the Crown and to MacMillan Bloedel

posed by the protestors could be clearly established. The map, like Clayoquot itself, was the ground of all arguments.

The specific map used as evidence in a court case is supposed to represent a commonly shared, objective understanding of the site of contention between two parties. Maps, however, are not objective; they represent cultural geographies.[8] A map is an interpretation of a set of relations between the mapper and the land. It does not represent all of the possible relations. As the foundational evidence crucial for an objective judgement, the map of TFL 44 was the cultural geography of MacMillan Bloedel. In other words, the mental framework from which the Clayoquot Sound protestors would be judged was to be MacMillan Bloedel's, because the authorities believed that this industrial giant's cultural geography was the common ground between the parties represented in court.

The map represented the industry's and the government's understanding of what Clayoquot Sound is: a timber supply area for which MacMillan Bloedel holds cutting rights to extract a resource. What the map did not show was that MacMillan Bloedel's surface title over public lands is only a residual relation to the land. First Nations, the Crown and the public hold prior title to the same land. The map of TFL 44 then became a definition of what is culturally legitimate, to the exclusion of all other cultural relations to the land. From the outset, exclusive reference to MacMillan Bloedel's map in court implied that only MacMillan Bloedel's title had standing in court. The court's use of the map of TFL 44 was therefore a graphic representation of an all-pervasive system of abuse.

In effect, the evidentiary map of TFL 44 excluded the cultural geographies of at least two other social groups. The first group is the First Nations inhabitants of Clayoquot Sound, the Nuu-chah-nulth people, who have continuously inhabited this ecosystem for over 4,800 years. The second group is the environmentalists.

Clayoquot Sound in the summer of 1993 came to mean much more than a timber supply to the thousands of people who arrived from all over and from every walk of life. Today, it continues to have especial meaning for the lives of some 930 people who chose to commit themselves to arrest in pacifist civil disobedience, in order to seek justice for all the inhabitants of the bio-community of Clayoquot Sound.[9] The meaning of the watersheds of Clayoquot Sound to these two groups differs radically from the industry's meaning.[10] For these groups, the watersheds represent the numinous power of cultural continuity dependent on the integrity of natural environments.

That the cultural geography of the industry embodied in the surface title is in reality subordinate, and yet imposes itself as the legitimate and unquestionable voice, leaving other cultural geographies unrecognized, is a manifestation of cultural rape. Industrial culture rapes not only the land but the cultures that inhabit it. By severing the sustainable relationship that prior cultures have held from time immemorial to the land, industrial culture destroys the sustainability of culture itself.[11]

Once the priority given to the dominant cultural map is removed, it becomes possible to give due weight to the rights of non-mainstream groups, and to preserve their identity. To begin, it will be helpful to look at the problem of rights in the context of First Nations. It will then be possible to recognize social and legal similarities between the First Nations' predicament and that faced by environmentalists as a dissenting group.

## Part III: The Recovery of Identity

The Canadian history of post-contact relations with First Nations is a sad record of abuse and cultural genocide. Foremost in that record is the arrogant, deliberate and relentless attempt forcefully to assimilate First Nations by means of the Indian Act (1876-1960), the avowed purpose of which was "to assimilate Native people to the Canadian mainstream."[12] This history of dispossession and land swindling, child abduction and abuse, has led to the dysfunctionality and criminalization of a large part of the First Nations population.[13]

It is essential that we understand that, for First Nations, the land and the people remain one. First Nations people consider their identity to be inextricably bound to the land. Although I cannot presume to speak for First Nations, I have come to appreciate what First Nations people mean when they say that their ancestors were not migrants from across the Bering Strait, but people born from the land. To a First Nations person, the house territory is "the centre of the world."[14] It is the centre of their cultural meaningfulness. There were no Zuni before the Zuni came to Zuni, no Dene before they came to Dene-da and there were no Haida before the Haida settled on Haida Gwai. The First Nations did not find the land; the land found them, because they had no meaning before the land gave them meaning. The destruction of the homeland is the destruction of their identity. Their cultural view indicates that it is not the individual who provides meaning, but the group as it has co-evolved with the place.

In British Columbia, the majority of First Nations have never ceded title to the land through treaty. What treaties *were* signed are subject to contradictory interpretations.[15] Prior title to the land has been, and continues to be, the object of First Nations' discussions of land claims with the government.[16] Most non-aboriginal people do not understand that aboriginal title should not be conceived in the same way that European culture has historically conceived the right to property. The European concept of property involves individual title to an object that the owner can dispose of as he or she sees fit. In other words, the ownership of a piece of land is like the ownership of a slave. The land has no claim to intrinsic value or rights anymore than does the slave; the owner has the absolute right to destroy it if he or she so desires. Destruction can in fact be viewed as an "improvement," because the act of destruction confirms the belief, however ill-founded, of the superiority of the property owner. The integrity of the property, be it land, slave or animal, is not a consideration. Destruction or improvement is then a reduction of the property to the satisfaction of the owner's ends. The doctrine of "improvement" of property confirms the legitimacy of sheer power and, as such, it affirms the subordination of any other conceivable intrinsic values to strictly human values.[17] This is what is known as a "proprietary interest."

Aboriginal title to the land is a radically different concept.[18] It is not a clear proprietary interest. Like aboriginal rights, aboriginal title must be understood within the parameters of the various aboriginal cultures. As Justice Lambert has noted, the question of whether the aboriginal title is or is not proprietary is misplaced, because this concept remains alien to the aboriginal relation to the land. An approach to this question through the jurisprudence of Anglo-American common law proves misleading, because no clear comparison exists in our legal tradition.[19]

Aboriginal relationship to the land is organismic. First Nations view the land as a living entity essential to the cultural identity of the people, not as an object of individual proprietary rights. Aboriginal title is a right to preserve the locus of cultural habitation. It is a collective or group right to the possession, use and enjoyment of the land, which can only be understood within the cultural norms of that group. After reviewing Canadian jurisprudence on this question, Justice Lambert states:

> ...aboriginal title is _sui generis_...it is neither entirely personal nor entirely proprietary. The meaning of _sui generis_ is that the thing so described is in a class or category of its own. It does not mean that the class or category is in any respect inferior to or lesser than any other class or category. The solution to further problems in relation to aboriginal title should be sought in a deeper understanding of the nature of the aboriginal title itself, _in aboriginal terms_, and not in attributing consequences under the common law on the basis that those consequences flow from a common law classification for tenure purposes of the aboriginal title or right as either proprietary or personal.[20]

Given the prior occupancy of the land by First Nations, from before the dawn of millenial oral traditions, aboriginal title modifies the Crown's absolute title because of its legal and historical antecedence. First Nations therefore have a clear prior legal claim to this land and any refusal to admit this is strictly political.[21]

In spite of their legitimate legal claim and the cultural and physical distinctiveness of the people, First Nations' rights continue to be contested by those who appeal to the doctrines of extinguishment and assimilation. Like assimilation, extinguishment presupposes that "Indianness" and claims based on a distinct cultural characteristic have either been relinquished voluntarily or by conquest. These twin concepts reinforce the prejudiced view that, in today's modern technological world, First Nations share in the global consumer culture, and are therefore not significantly culturally distinct.[22] The desired assimilation that was not achieved through the Indian Act is then assumed to have been fulfilled by a *fiat*, or voice of power. To acquiesce to this reasoning is to endorse the legitimacy of the myth of monoculture. Technological society's mental map continues to form a perceptive wall that guards its privileges.[23]

Three key considerations arise from the legal reality of the First Nations' claim. First, cultural integrity depends on the integrity of the land and therefore precedes the commonly accepted proprietary interests. The recognition of aboriginal title as having priority over the Crown title, limits the right of surface-title holders to despoil the land beyond the point that despoilment would destroy the foundation of the culture.

Second, recognition of aboriginal rights entails the recognition of the special character of group rights within the *Canadian Constitutional Act* (1982), as witnessed in sections 15, ii, and section 35.

Third, aboriginal claims to title indicate that claims other than the proprietary or usufructory claims commonly understood in the Anglo-American common law tradition can be entertained. Thus, usufructory claims that assume the priority interests of visible users or "improvers" over the claims of less visible or low-impact users do not have a legitimate priority. Usufructory rights characterize the colonial view that the land was a "desert" when it was in fact inhabited by First Nations who did not despoil the land, but instead made full use of it. Proprietary rights and industrial usufruction are not the only ways of understanding the cultural relation one has to the land, and therefore are not the only forms of legitimate entitlement.

Given that aboriginal title "is a burden on the root title of the Crown,"[24] our view of the land and our relation to it as new inhabitants of this continent ought to be consistent with the obligations to preserve the land as the locus of culture that is entailed in that burden. Consequently, proprietary interests must take into account the implications of the land as a living entity, which may then be considered to have jural standing.[25]

The First Nations' defense of their cultures can be made only by representatives of the various First Nations. By pointing to their distinctiveness from "white society," aboriginal peoples over the last three decades have made giant steps in recovering from the cultural rape of the last five hundred years.[26] In Canada, the acceptance of this distinctiveness becomes possible only because the nation is a "cultural mosaic." Therefore, the recognition of the inherent character of distinct social groups is a commonly accepted article of faith, even if the historical practice of discrimination and racism belies this.

A group's recovery of identity in a technological society is not a problem limited to aboriginal cultures. Recognition of the dysfunctionality of technological society is key to the recovery of identity.[27] Given that First Nations stand at the very end of the social spectrum, the social ills that characterize their dysfunctionality—such as family violence, substance dependency, youth suicide, and low self esteem—are in fact indicators of our social condition. Their plight resembles that of canaries in a mineshaft. If they are in trouble, we are in trouble. The presence of dissenting groups signals that there is a growing consciousness of the critical situation we face collectively. But the socially mature admission of that fact is achieved only if we recognize the legitimacy of the distinctive vision of dissenting groups.

That environmentalists comprise a distinct group with cultural similarities to First Nations, may seem difficult at first to accept. Since environmentalists are neither a visible nor religious minority, people assume that environmentalists operate within the cultural geography of mainstream North America. Yet Western or "white" society is a highly complex and diverse web of social geographies that brings together three spheres of existence that are the objects of rights: the individual, the group and society. Each individual is socialized within a group, and each group contributes to the fabric of society. These three spheres of existence are interdependent. The dignity of human life is inconceivable without the interplay of these three spheres of being. Just as no individual can impose his or her will on a democracy, no single group can claim to be the voice of society as a whole. Nevertheless, technocratic corporate cultural mapping assumes it can be the sole voice, and in this assumption it violates the rights of both individuals and groups. To a great extent, this violation occurs because corporate culture heightens the proprietary rights founded on a strong sense of individualism that pervades constitutional history.[28] It emphasizes the polarity between the individual and society, thereby excluding communal considerations.

First Nations people and environmentalists oppose the hegemony of technocratic corporate culture by appealing to their own group distinctiveness. Not surprisingly, although they remain separate, they share a common historical moment. The American Indian Movement and the Radical Environmental Movement find their roots in the nineteenth century, but crystallize as a political cultural entity bent on the recovery of their cultural identity in the 1960s and early '70s.[29] This ideological and temporal convergence has led to common positions regarding environmental issues.[30] In spite of these affinities it would be erroneous to convert environmentalists into a tribe of Wannabes. They constitute a distinct group of dissidents. Their common ecocentric perspective creates ideological similarities with First Nations regarding the rights of the land, group identity, and participatory democracy.[31] These similarities also leave environmentalists open to the same system of societal abuses.

The common ground between First Nations and environmentalists lies in the recognition of the earth as a living entity. Environmentalists represent both a new and old tradition within

Western culture, just as ecology is both an old and new science. The novelty lies in the re-emergence of ancient sensibilities in a modern context.

We live in a world of changing timescales. We have only lately come to realize that the human presence on earth is a short 15 minutes in a global year of 365 days. Similarly, the reality created by the technological culture we have endorsed as "the real" or "commonsense" condition of man is a recent departure from both the universal history of mankind and Western civilization itself. The hegemony of technocratic society, which we have witnessed since the end of the Second World War, must be understood to be only one aspect of Western culture. Technology—the application of mechanistic tendencies of the seventeenth-century's Scientific Revolution—has achieved its dominant position largely as a result of the demographic reorganization of the Industrial Revolution in nineteenth-century Europe.[32] The prescriptive character of industrial technology harnessed human energy to the needs of the machine, and thus the world came to be perceived as a machine.[33] Environmentalists represent a time-honoured social alternative to the relatively recent hegemony of technological ideology.

Technology and ecology as cultural mindsets are deeply rooted in separate strands of Western culture. Their origins are found simultaneously in contradictory documents that have shaped our culture. Although the technological view of man has Biblical antecedents, the Bible itself is a contradictory document which at times provided an organismic understanding of the world.[34] It is therefore not surprising that during and after the Scientific Revolution a long and respectable scientific and philosophical tradition continued which upheld an organismic view of the earth, which came in part from the Biblical tradition of seventeenth-century divines.[35]

The organismic tradition has received renewed vigour with the development of ecology, particularly in the work of three scientists, Frederic Clements (1874-1945), Aldo Leopold (1886-1948) and J.E. Lovelock (b. 1919). In 1928, Clements articulated a demonstrable hypothesis, known as the climax theory, which proposed that ecosystems were "superorganisms."[36] Aldo Leopold realized that, given the animate character of the land, human beings—if they were to survive and to preserve their humanity—had to re-assess their relationship to the land. To that end, he formulated a "land ethic" in 1948.[37] The land ethic was a crucial move in recognizing the intrinsic value of every living species and in removing the priority of human beings in the valuation of other beings who share this planet. In 1979, J.E. Lovelock confirmed the organismic insight by providing a coordinated scientific theory, known as the Gaia hypothesis: that the earth itself functions as a single organism.[38]

Environmentalism is therefore one of the faces of Western culture. It belongs to a lengthy, if minority, tradition within Western culture that has reflected humanity's condition within nature. As such, radical environmentalism is not a revolt against culture; it affirms culture. One finds its historical and cultural place within the liberal and democratic tradition of natural rights and pluralism. Every aspect of radical environmentalism finds its roots in the tradition of Magna Carta. Not surprisingly, environmentalism is part of the North-American psyche, and has flourished in North-American society.[39] As Roderick Nash has noted: "the environmental movement can be understood not so much as a revolt against traditional American ideals as an extension and new application of them."[40] The technological culture, however, has a long and grizzly totalitarian tradition.[41]

Environmentalists therefore constitute a group intent on retrieving a cultural inheritance that has been largely destroyed by a severance from the land brought about by an overdependence on technology. In focussing on the inherent value, and attempting to speak on behalf of the rights of the land, they reassert values that lie at the heart of culture. The ecological view of the land provides a set of ultimate meanings that give environmentalists a sense of communality, within which they can establish an identity founded on democratic ideals.

# Part IV:  Alienations and Perceptions

If environmentalism is an integral part of Western culture, then we must answer why and how it is marginalized. This problem has two aspects. The first, which will be the subject of this section, is sociological. The second is the legal marginalization of environmentalists, to be discussed in Part V.

The marginalization of environmentalism is the result of the co-option of science by industrial technology. Two views of science have always co-existed, but only one has meaning for technological society. That meaning is conveyed and controlled by the media. The double bind of environmentalism can be understood by considering its relation to science and the media.

Environmentalists diverge from mainstream Western culture in their opposition to a reductive interpretation of "science" as the pursuit of the management of nature to further the interests of industrial society. Technology's "hard" view of science is a desire for absolute control. The values environmentalists aspire to are shaped by the holistic insights of the contemporary science of ecology. "Soft" science is a non-reductive inquiry into appropriate mutualist relationships and interdependence of all beings.

Whereas the strictly socio-cultural foundation of the First Nations' claim to identity has traditionally been marginalized by the so-called "scientific claims" of the myth of technological progress, the scientific foundation of environmentalism poses a direct challenge to the predominant scientific claims of industrial culture. Technological control of nature and humans succeeds only so long as one does not inquire beyond the narrow focus of technology. Hard science never questions its technological frame of reference, and thus it limits itself to quantification and creates the illusion of exactitude and control. The role that hard science plays in a technological culture is instrumental in limiting debate.[42]

Technology is only one application of science; it is not, as governments and industry revel in telling us, "science."[43] Science is concerned with bold investigation of the reality beyond the confines of accepted views. To be science, it must forever question the limits of its metaphysical views and accept the provisional character of its applications. Technology is the unquestioning application, or verification, of a metaphysical view that claims to be the only view, and thereby becomes a dogma, as clearcutting has in industrial forestry.[44] Science inquires, technology does not. It uses science as a means to an end, without questioning that end.

This comparison of the differing environmental and technological uses of science is vital to understand the complexity of the Clayoquot debate. The official marginalization of the "soft" approach to science raises a problem of public perception, both of the issue itself and of the environmentalists as a social group, because hard science and public perception pervade every aspect of the manufacturing of "official" truth. The Clayoquot Decision of April 13th 1993 could only be endorsed by a public who believed that the decision had scientific credibility, that science/technology could keep all problems under control, and that the industry could continue business as usual, with no serious repercussions.

The problem of scientific credibility affects the twin questions of how the Clayoquot Decision was arrived at, and how the environmentalists who took part in the protests were viewed. As the only School of Forestry in the province until recently, the University of British Columbia's Forestry Faculty has effectively controlled the destiny of forest policy in this province. Its orientation has always been corporate. In the last decade, relations with the industry have increased.[45] Corporate involvement in university funding and policy has undermined the freedom of academic research. The appointment of the President of U.B.C. to the Board of MacMillan Bloedel, and the Dean of Forestry to that of West Fraser Timber, and of senior faculty members such as J.P. Kimmins to The Forest Alliance narrows the proximate interests of the university and the corporations. Thus, the (until recently) Senior Vice-President, Research and Development, of MacMillan Bloedel, Otto Forgacs, has stated that if the corporations fund research, they have the right to determine what research is relevant, because corporations are the voice of society. In the words of Otto Forgacs:

There is freedom of expression, there is freedom of the press, and there is freedom that I'm less than sympathetic to, that is [freedom] to do research whether it is going to contribute to society or not.[46]

In this climate, the research atmosphere has been altered radically towards technological and corporate ends, as witnessed by the twenty-year experience of John Carlson, a biotechnologist in the Forestry Faculty:

The research climate is a lot different now than it was 20 years ago when science was for the purpose of uncovering new knowledge and seeing how the world was made. Now it's primarily directed towards short term goals that have economic benefits.[47]

Under the guise of science, corporate and academic use of technology is a practical pursuit of power for political ends.

Under normal conditions, a political decision such as the Clayoquot Decision is arrived at by consultation with corporate, government, independent and university scientists. Ideally, the process should be impartial.[48] In a system in which all four voices are formed by the university, under the aegis of corporate research, one has grounds to question the impartiality of perspectives. Here again, in the scientific sphere, the industry's voice poses as the only legitimate frame of reference, as the voice of society. The environmental voice is discredited as not belonging to the official voice of science, when in fact the voice of science has been usurped by corporate technology. Thus, at every level of discourse one finds that the corporate voice dominates the flow of information.

As a consequence of their displacement from a legitimate place within scientific discourse, environmentalists are perceived by the public as individuals who oppose science and progress. Presented as enemies of official science, they allegedly pose a threat to the well-being of the community.[49] Again, human progress is confused with the progress of technology. As a result, the limitation of knowledge masquerades as the pursuit of truth and freedom. The marginalization of environmentalists is further heightened when their challenge to technological hegemony is interpreted as a challenge to the industrial economy and employment.

Technology becomes the focal point and source of values because it promises an escape from environmental limitations brought about by abuse. Technology proposes that human beings can dispense with nature, can create improved environments that surpass the limits of the earth's carrying capacity.[50] Technology is therefore tied to the promise of endless production to satisfy endless wants. Whether it be in a Marxist or a capitalist economy, technology as the means to endless production in an industrial economy becomes an end in itself. Far from liberating humans, it increases their vulnerability, multiplying the individual's dependency on an economy of endless wants and his or her reliance on specialists to provide for these wants.[51] Reliance limits the real freedom of individuals. The technological society is one of prescriptive control. Contrary to popular belief, control need not be coercion. It takes two passive forms. Control is structured within an economy, because an economy is by definition a set of interdependent limiting relations. Different economies allow different degrees of freedom. Furthermore, supreme control depends on the management of information.

The technological mindset affects the public's perception of environmentalists because the media packages acceptable images for public assimilation. Public relations therefore assume a crucial role in controlling that image. As in the case of the public perception of aboriginals, the media translates events and the cultural realities of groups from within technological discourse. It therefore develops an image that responds to the cultural expectations of technological culture, and in this manner the media creates mainstream environmentalism.

Given the power of the media to shape public perceptions, control of the media is a political necessity in the pursuit of power. Public-relations firms are hired to sell the corporate truth by filtering information and tailoring the message for public consumption. In the Clayoquot debate, disinformation was the role of Burson-Marsteller, the notorious public-relations corporation best known for its cover-ups of Bhopal, the Argentinian dirty war, etc., hired by MacMillan Bloedel. Its political function in organizing the entire network of media opposition to environmentalism, the SHARE B.C. groups, The Forest Alliance, and the press itself, is well-documented. Burson-Marsteller took on the job of social engineering that is a structural part of technological society, consistent with its anti-democratic orientation.[52]

But to understand Clayoquot as a cultural issue we should not be blinded by the political issues it also raised. Political issues only shed light on the society that dominated the flow of information. To concentrate on this is to fail to move beyond technocracy's narrow focus, and not to understand the cultural position of environmentalism. Important as it is, the role of Burson-Marsteller is a political externality that causes us to overlook the deep-set problems that arise from the technological character of the media itself. As an inherent part of technological culture, media plays an important passive role in neutralizing the power of environmental culture.

In this discussion of the media's attempts to present environmentalism, we should not overlook the environmental movement's own contradictory relationship to the media. Given the predominantly non-violent and consciousness-raising orientation of environmental causes, the environmentalists are forced to depend on media attention. This is necessary because a high proportion of environmental actions and concerns take place in locations so remote that without media presence the vast majority of the population would remain unaware of them. Although the media orientation of environmental action brings forth a positive response, the message of the media itself belongs to the disconnected character of modern technological life and remains a clinical two-minute sound bite. By the time this information reaches the average North-American home, it has been packaged for the very consumption that the action was intent on opposing. The media's focus, even when it intends to be provocative, remains characteristically narrow, so that it can never truly challenge the presuppositions of the viewer.

A public event such as the Clayoquot summer, in which a vast number of people participated, and which generated the largest mass arrest in Canadian history, poses special difficulties for consumption. To present its full complexity the media would have to put into question the underpinnings of technological culture and the very existence of media consumerism.

What the media could not handle at Clayoquot was the grassroots character of the event. Pacifist, well-ordered and moving as the mass arrest of August 9th was, its grassroots power could not be communicated to a consumer public. The focus of the eye of the camera is always selective and clinical, even before the film is edited. The human urgency and power could not be communicated to a public already desensitized by information overload. The efficiency and force of the environmental movement lies in its participatory democratic character. To make the event understandable to the public, the media had to translate it into hierarchic terms. To this effect it focussed not on the people as a whole, that is as a group, but on the individuals "in charge." The media directed its attention to categories it knew: "organizers," "leaders," "environmental groups and corporations" that corresponded to the corporate structure easily assimilable by the public. In so doing, it undermined the participatory, grassroots identity of the protest. In effect, the media assumed control of the protest to bring it into mainstream thinking. This is not a new phenomenon in environmental culture.[53] By initiating the process of mainstreaming, the media takes control of the cultural meaning of the group. As in the colonial practice of "speaking for" First Nations, the media becomes the voice of environmentalism. It initiates the process of reconfiguring the cultural mapping of information, effectively destroying the group character of the protest by focussing on the externalities. In so doing, it avoids a recognition of the group's legitimate cultural structure and claims. Hence, issues presented to the public become confined to categories familiar to the viewers: "trees, jobs and loggers." The event is raped of its inherent cultural significance.

One of the aspects of media assimilation was the presentation of the Clayoquot Protest as a kind of "freak show." Like any other consumer item, the protest was touted for its novelty within a pre-existing category. It was advertised as the "Woodstock of the 90's," packaged as a generation gap "anarchist holiday."[54] As another Woodstock, the Clayoquot was easily associated with kids, drugs, sex, tribalism, as well as social experimentation. Here the media was at odds with reality. "Raging Grannies," blind people, priests, teachers, nurses, loggers and foresters—in fact all types and ages came to be arrested. Moreover, the Peace Camp's code forbade the presence and use of drugs and alcohol.

To understand Clayoquot we have to move beyond the media's constraints. In trying to marginalize the cultural importance of Clayoquot by hyping the novel character of the protest, the media failed to understand or even acknowledge the thought-provoking precedents that might make it intelligible to the public.

A mass public event such as Woodstock does not possess the kind of solid ideological foundation that one finds in the phenomenon of the Clayoquot Protest. As a result it is ephemeral, and can be aped but never repeated, because it does not have a culturally-determined sense of purpose and direction. That is the difference between a social protest and a cultural affirmation of rights through protest, such as Clayoquot.

The Clayoquot Protest was in itself nothing new. Without detracting from the abilities and determination of the original group of the Friends of Clayoquot, who had been involved in protests for more than a decade, one needs to note that the 1993 protest drew together an environmental grassroots community that acted within an established tradition of radical environmental protest. Without that communality, there would have been no effective protest. The Clayoquot protest repeated an environmental formula of Gandhian non-violent group protest initiated two decades before in 1970, in the Mardola Falls protest in Norway, that was then tested in British Columbia on smaller scales at the Stein Valley, South Moresby, Carmanah Valley, Lilloet Lake and the Walbran Valley. The Mardola Falls protest was largely the brainchild of Norwegian deep ecology philosophers Sigmund Kvaloy, Finn Alnaes and Arne Naess. The well-worked-out philosophical lineage of environmental protests gives them a tradition based on the realization that the depth of our current global predicament can no longer be addressed within the conventional paradigms of modern industrial and technological society.

Deep ecology is an attempt to reconnect selfhood and sense of place within their cultural matrix. It is one of the few philosophical approaches which returns to the origins of Greek philosophy by posing the ontological question of how one ought *to be* in the world.[55] Deep ecology distinguishes itself from reform ecology by considering the intrinsic importance of nature and the human relation to nature in its plenitude, rather than the preservation of nature for the maintenance of the health and affluence of people in developed countries.[56] Deep ecology possesses a sense of bio-egalitarianism, which extends to the praxis of social justice. It is not a systematic philosophy, but an individually-oriented approach to re-conceiving the nature of being within a pluralist ethic. In this respect, it places strong demands on the local and communal character of relations that shape the pluralist reality of our ecological condition.[57] The non-hierarchic character of ecocentric thought inserts deep ecology within the non-violent tradition of Gandhian thought and, therefore, within the Western tradition of pacifist civil disobedience.[58]

Thus, the Mardola Falls Protest of 1970 was the practical application of the philosophy of deep ecology. Mardola Falls, a spectacular 2,000-foot cascade in central Norway, was slated to be dammed. The project consituted a violation of the environmental heritage of the traditionally outdoor-oriented Norwegian culture. It is no surprise that the protest was organized by some of the country's leading intellectuals. It was a pacifist reaction guided by a code of non-violence, and structured around a Peace Camp welcoming all people concerned. The organizers were of course the first to commit themselves to arrest, in order to argue their case in court with courtesy and great respect for the law, in keeping with the Gandhian tradition. This same formula, which was used throughout Europe, principally in anti-nuclear protests, was repeated in Norway on a much larger scale in the Alta River Protest of 1979-1980, with the formation of a provisional Green village. With the successful introduction of deep ecology as a philosophical discipline in America throughout the eighties, and the radicalization of environmentalism through the Reagan years, deep ecology and Mardola Falls became the formulae for environmental protests of the late eighties, and crystallized on a large scale American version, in the massive "Redwood Summer" of California in 1990.

The Clayoquot Sound Protest was to a large extent a repetition of Redwood Summer, articulating locally the same concerns over industrial rape of the forest and its social impact. Interested only in the image, the media omitted all mention of these foundations and precedents, and in so doing took possession of the event and denied the cultural voice of environmental groups. The media thereby legitimized the systematic practice of cultural rape, and silenced dissidence by assuming its voice. The group identity of environmentalists therefore does not lie in the image made of it. As in the case of aboriginal culture, the identity of environmental culture may best be understood in legal parameters.

## Part V:   Environmental Group Rights

As a result of media-packaging, the public tends to see environmentalists merely as a political group, in the same way that it conceives of the cultural aspirations of First Nations as political challenges. Once it is recognized, however, that environmentalists are motivated by a deeply held set of beliefs determined by a distinct understanding of the ontological status of humans, other species and landforms, they can then be seen as a cultural, not merely a political reality. As in the case of First Nations, environmentalism is a different manner of conceiving the world, and what being in the world means. The legitimacy of the environmentalists' claim to group rights is vindicated, not only by the historical continuity of ecocentrism, but by the vulnerability of environmental interests to abuse by mainstream interests. This vulnerability becomes entrenched in the adversarial character of the legal process.

The central consideration in the claim to the distinct group rights of both environmentalists and First Nations is the ecocentric character of their cultural beliefs. Given the parallels and precedents created by the legitimacy of First Nations' claims regarding right relation to the land, the aspirations of environmentalists ought to be approached *sui generis*. The *sui generis* aspect of the claim arises from the distinct relationship that environmentalists have with the land.

If environmentalists can be considered as a dissident cultural group with rights to the exercise of beliefs distinct from the mainstream, and which still forms part of Canadian society, then several questions regarding that relationship must be considered. First, what are their legitimate expectations, and can they be addressed within the "reasonable limits prescribed by law" (section 1) in the *Canadian Charter of Rights and Freedoms?* Second, to what extent do these legitimate expectations disadvantage them in society and make them vulnerable? Third, can their expectations be met without resorting to civil disobedience? What remedies are available to them, and to what extent may pacifist civil disobedience be legitimate under the *Charter of Rights and Freedoms?*

These problems can be addressed only within the context of legal precedents resting on the close association between freedom of conscience and religion. Environmental beliefs are based on a scientific and secular foundation. The fact that these beliefs are teleological gives them a quasi-religious character. The distinctiveness and legitimacy of these beliefs is reinforced by their affinity with First Nations' cultural beliefs, which are entrenched in the fabric of Canadian life through both section 39 of the *Charter,* and the manner in which the precedence of aboriginal title affects the special character of and relationship to the land.

In Canada, no cultural group can impose its beliefs and practices on another. That all cultural groups are equal was the object of a ruling of the Supreme Court of Canada on the Ontario government's attempt to prevent Sunday shopping in the case of *Regina v Big M Drug Mart Ltd.*, [1985] 1 S.C.R. 870. This ruling

> protects against all state-imposed burdens on the exercise of religious beliefs, whether direct and indirect, intentional or unintentional, foreseeable or unforeseeable, provided they cannot be regarded as merely trivial or insubstantial.[59]

This ruling guarantees cultural groups immunity from laws that interfere with a way of life and provides for "justification for activities that would otherwise be unlawful."[60] Although cases covered by this ruling appeal principally to religious matters of conscience, the separation of "conscience" and "religion" in the Charter gives greater breadth of application in instances regarding secular conscience. This is particularly relevant in environmental cases, given the ambivalent character of the secular quality of the beliefs held by the group.

The exercise of environmental beliefs depends upon the preservation of wilderness, which is the locus of environmental meaning. This position is not trivial; it is based on a well-substantiated concern for ecocide. In principle, environmental groups could demand that their cultural beliefs call for the preservation of wilderness areas like Clayoquot Sound. But such a demand would run up against the limiting clause in our constitution. Fundamental freedoms are

> subject only to such reasonable limits prescribed by law as can be demonstrably justified in a free and democratic society.
>
> (Canadian Charter of Rights and Freedoms, section 1)

The limitation is on what is intended by "reasonable." The problem of determining what is meant by "reasonability" opens onto the perennial contention that surrounds the concept of Reason. Reason is itself a cultural construct that mirrors certain human interests. If Reason is something that humans share, then it ought to benefit all parties. Interestingly, conduct that threatens us with ecocide may seem rational to a benefiting party, but cannot be considered rational if it does not benefit all parties, including the nonhuman parties.

Just as there can be no single, or monist, comprehensive picture of reality, but only a plurality of approximations to reality, so too there is no single Reason, but a shared plurality of reasons. The pluralist character of environmental logic contrasts radically with the monist character of the law conceived as positive law, that is, as the application of prescriptive rules. Problems emanating from the exercise of a monist Reason are further exacerbated by the fact that the Anglo-American legal tradition is not characterized by positive law, but by a pluralist recourse to custom and precedence, entrenched in the tradition of natural law as the cornerstone of our constitutional heritage.[61]

In the Clayoquot trials, by grounding its judgements strictly on the basis of positive law, and overlooking natural law which has precedence, the court adopted a political position consistent with the prescriptive and anti-democratic orientation of technological society. The court then became the voice of technological society and marginalized its dissidents.

The problem of "reasonable limits" has important ramifications concerning the applications of "reasonableness" as a test in the Clayoquot trials, both through the Charter's explicit limitation of freedoms and as a limitation of possible defenses for disobeying an injunction. Reasonableness is a fundamental consideration in the problem of rights because there must be reasonably demonstrable grounds for the exercise of a right. This consideration pitches the monist interpretation of Reason as a shared cultural image against the pluralist question of whose reason, or which cultural map, has priority in court?

To understand how axial this question is when considering the legal predicament of environmentalists, one needs to consider how the scientific basis of the environmentalists' beliefs makes them vulnerable in court. As in all environmental cases, what is reasonable in law is not necessarily reasonable in science, and vice versa. Law and science are two different systems of logic. One therefore finds that a monist approach to the law becomes a political, rather than strictly legal position, in support of dominant cultural interests that marginalize group rights. To counter this inclination, the legal tradition gives considerable latitude to the interpretation of "reasonable." Thus, in the interpretation of *The Charter* the guiding principle is the well-known statement of Lord Hailsham:

> Two reasonable [persons] can perfectly reasonably come to opposite conclusions on the same set of facts without forfeiting their title to be reasonable... Not every reasonable exercise of judgment is right, and not every mistaken exercise of judgment is unreasonable. There is a band of decisions within which no court should seek to replace the individual's judgment with his own.[62]

In the Clayoquot trials the court injunctions replaced individual judgment on the grounds that no reasonable person would oppose an order in court, and that any reasonable person would have sought alternative remedies within the law, such as challenging the injunction or suing MacMillan Bloedel.[63]

The cultural beliefs of the environmentalists posed a dilemma in court. The government's criminalization of the injunction faced environmentalists with two reasonable sets of facts: the scientific/cultural facts and the legal facts. Given the cultural nature of the contention, the Attorney General's intervention placed the judiciary in the untenable position of replacing individual judgment and violating conscience. It is therefore crucial to understand the difficult position in which the courts were placed by the Attorney General and by the structural limitations of the adversarial character of the legal process.

The Attorney General's abuse of his advantageous position within the limitations of the adversarial process lies at the heart of the Clayoquot arrests. The protestors were engaged in a civil dispute between themselves and MacMillan Bloedel. MacMillan Bloedel sought and obtained an injunction to enable it to proceed against the protestors, individually, in a civil suit. The Attorney General of B.C. intervened on behalf of MacMillan Bloedel to proceed against the protestors as a group in a criminal trial. The reasonable contention between two parties then became a prosecution with only one rationale having standing, that of the government and the industry.

Given that the source of rights is not the government but the people, the environmentalists involved in the protest felt that they had certain legitimate claims in court. The central claim was freedom from ecocide. Regarding that constitutional right, Harry Pettigrew has stated:

> With the pervasive and impersonal nature of the big government-business-industry complex and enormity and severity of ecological problems it is essential that courts act as *custodes* and provide the individual with effective legal vehicles for the protection of his interests in a decent environment.[64]

Although redress sought by the environmentalists should have been available, either by initiating a civil suit against MacMillan Bloedel or by initiating challenges to the injunction in court, the environmental nature of the situation posed certain structural problems that limited these courses of action. In addition to the problems of proceeding while the logging continued, and the cost of initiating individual legal action, there is a structural legal consideration that *obliges* environmentalists to engage in pacifist civil disobedience.

Given their disadvantaged position, the environmentalists found the political avenue foreclosed once the government introduced the Clayoquot Decision. Quite simply, by the time the matter was resolved and any political remedy achieved, Clayoquot would be logged so extensively that its special ecosystemic character would be lost. There was good reason as well for the environmentalists not to undertake a liability suit against MacMillan Bloedel. The adversarial character of a liability suit disadvantages environmental plaintiffs, no matter how valid their scientific evidence may be. Burden of proof in scientific discourse which depends on a balance of probabilities, is distinct from burden of proof in legal discourse, where it depends on proof of proximate cause. In the adversarial legal system, the name of the game is to be a defendant. As MacMillan Bloedel's record of violations shows, the real criminals always win. The environmental plaintiff is in the difficult, if not impossible position of matching scientific burden of proof with legal burden of proof. It is therefore strategically important for disadvantaged parties to take the role of defendants by breaking a law that protects the offending party. In taking the role of a defendant, the position of an environmentalist is stronger, and the purported harm caused by the plaintiff (such as MacMillan Bloedel) can be exposed, thereby legitimizing the activity of the defendant as a matter of necessity or justification. The advantageous strategic role of the defendant explains why, although corporations such as MacMillan Bloedel retaliate by initiating SLAPPs (Strategic Lawsuits Against Public Participation) to intimidate members of the public, they rarely proceed against the defendants. What would come out in court would be damning for the plaintiff.[65]

The intent of the Clayoquot protestors was to have MacMillan Bloedel take the role of the plaintiff in a civil contention, _without the political protection of the government._ It is a customary recourse in a civil dispute to break the law in order to vindicate one's legal rights.[66] In breaking the Salt Laws, Gandhi was able to reveal the iniquities of the colonial government in India. This custom is part of the checks and balances against government or corporate abuse guaranteed by the neutrality of the judiciary. That balance is necessary to give all groups an equal voice. However, the theoretical balance is offset in practice by the structural problem of _proximate cause._ It is a legal problem that further affects the vulnerability of environmentalists in court.

The key difficulty in bringing out the malfeasance of corporations like MacMillan Bloedel is a well-known problem of showing immediate causal relationship between the activity of the defendant and the harm claimed by the plaintiff. If the harm is somehow remote or hypothetical, the law considers that it is not satisfactorily demonstrable. Good science is always hypothetical, and therefore carries little weight in law. Good technology always claims to be in control of causal relations, and has therefore good standing in law. This is the doctrine of proximate cause which opposes scientific proof against legal proof. The political nature of the obstruction was established in 1928 by Justice Andrews in *Palsgraaf v Long Island Railroad* [248 NY, 339, 352, 162 NE 99, 103 (1928)]:

> The scientist's mistrust of the legal system perhaps stems from frustration of showing harm and causation, yet losing the case because the cause in fact is deemed—arbitrarily it seems—not significant enough to hold the defendant legally responsible. His frustrations are further compounded when he learns that no amount of factual analysis can surmount this barrier because the question of proximate cause is one of legal policy.... Proximate cause is a form of line beyond which liability will not extend, it is a question of law, rather than one of fact (as stated by Justice Andrews): "What we do mean by the word *proximate* is, that because of convenience, of public policy, *of a rough sense of justice*, the law arbitrarily declines to trace a series of events beyond a certain point. *This is not logic. This is practical politics.*"[67]

In *Palsgraaf,* Justice Andrews was adjudicating a matter of pollution. In 1928, environmental problems had not galvanized group consciousness. However, environmental crises have now reached such proportions and intensity that environmental consciousness has acquired a cultural coherence that distinguishes it from mainstream technocratic and industrial society. The doctrine of proximate cause then contributes to infringements on the rights of conscience and the rights of dissenting groups.

In the Clayoquot trials, the implications of proximate cause greatly alter the relevance of the political intention. While the court was bound to weigh the proximate cause of an apparent claim to work stoppage occasioned by the blockade of Kennedy River Bridge, it refused to look beyond the proximate cause to the dangers posed by the activities of MacMillan Bloedel, by denying the validity of defenses of justification or necessity. Instead, the court fulfilled the practical ends of the Attorney General on behalf of MacMillan Bloedel, within the boundaries of legal policy. In this way, the court did not address the legitimate concerns of protestors, to whom it had equal obligations.

In the Clayoquot trials, reliance on the doctrine of proximate cause has meant that the rights of the people, and most notably those of a class of individuals known as "environmentalists," have become subordinate to a political end.[68] One must take into account the vulnerability of environmentalists through both the limitations of group rights and their structural exclusion as dissidents from adequate protection of the law. In theory, group rights are protected under section 15, subsection ii, of the *Charter*, even though they are ill-defined as a subset of individual rights:

> 15 i.  Every individual is equal before or under the law and has the right to equal protection and benefit of the law without discrimination....

> 15 ii.  Subsection (1) does not preclude any law, program or activity that has as its object the amelioration of conditions of disadvantaged individuals or groups....

The fact that subsection ii sanctions activities which help disadvantaged groups seems to place pacifist civil disobedience in the legal sphere. As a legally disadvantaged group seeking the amelioration of conditions necessary to its cultural identity, environmentalists have a right to engage in pacifist civil disobedience as a legitimate activity to improve their condition.

A major problem throughout the Clayoquot trials was the group character of the offense. Whereas each protestor viewed his or her action as a matter of individual conscience, the Crown and the courts (following the definition of the gravamen of "criminal contempt," as stated by Madame Justice McLachlin in *United Nurses of Alberta v. Attorney General of Alberta* [1992]) viewed the protest as a collective act, a group action characterized by its "public nature," because "the accused defied or disobeyed a court order in a public way."[69] "Public way" means that there were at least two persons present: an actor and a witness to the act.

This leads to an important paradox. Whereas the court condemned the protestors as a group, their group rights were not considered. If it was a group action, and the court reiterated in its judgments that a group was involved, then the group needed to be identified and defined, to determine its collective rights.

At present, the courts seem to view the concept of group rights as inimical to positive law. They view group action as "mob rule," as a collective pursuit inimical to societal norms and individual freedom. Yet our very humanity lies in our communal participation:

> Communality is the ground of a right—the right of groups to maintain themselves and to pursue distinctive courses because communality is one of the characteristic structures of existence, and in that sense, of the intrinsic human good. To rob existence of communality, of the communal celebratory process which forms the substance of much of our experience, would be to deny one ethical constituent of our humanity.[70]

The difficulty in the courts' acceptance of environmentalists' rights arises from the fact that the constitution defines freedoms and democratic rights (as opposed to legal rights) in positive and acquisitive terms, as guaranteed *freedoms to*. The right sought by environmentalists is a *freedom from*. As dissidents within a society of consumption, environmentalists are denied freedom from the power of consumption. If the technological ethos of consumerism poses a threat to our humanity, as social thinkers such as Postman contend, then it is understandable that group rights affirming our humanity appear inimical to a legal system representative of prevalent societal norms.

The right to be free from consumerism is symmetrical to the right to an environment free from degradation. In fact, this right is presupposed in the right to security of life guaranteed in section 7 of *The Charter*. Protection of the environment is therefore essential to the preservation of identity of a class of individuals known as environmentalists, who have a legitimate cultural claim. However, environmentalists are structurally vulnerable within the law because, historically, their rights have always been obliged to cede to the prerogatives of consumers. The rights of a group that makes exploitive demands will always override those of a group that makes sustainable demands. When people view the land as a commodity to which they have a proprietary claim, rather than as a living entity to which they have obligations, they then assume that those who do not abuse the land make insufficient use of it, those who abuse it maximize its benefit to mankind.

What such a view of the land means within the Anglo-American adversarial court system has been clearly set out as far back as 1970 by Professor Krier:

> Burden of proof rules at present have an inevitable bias against protection of the environment and preservation of natural resources. This is the case for the following reasons: Essentially two classes of demands can be made on such resources as air, land, water, wildlife and so on 1) demands that consume and deteriorate those resources... 2) demands that do not consume. In a world without laws, those who wish to use resources for consumptive or deteriorating ends will always prevail, over those who wish to use them for nonconsumptive or deteriorating ends. This is simply because consuming users, by exercising their demands, can foreclose the nonconsuming users from exercising theirs, while the contrary is not true. In short, the polluter's use can stop the swimmer from using and enjoying the lake, but the swimmer's [use] cannot stop the polluter from polluting the lake.
>
> Of course, we live in a system of laws, but it is a loaded system. And it is loaded precisely because of the point I have just made. For even in a world with rules against resource consumption...the leverage inherent in resource consumers means that they will continue their conduct until sued. In short, they will almost inevitably be *defendants* and those whose uses preserve rather than deteriorate will ineluctably be *plaintiffs*. And it is one of the simple facts of our present system that...plaintiffs most generally carry the burden of proving the most basic issues in a lawsuit. *The result is striking: Even with a system of substantive rules against resource consumption, our present rules ensure that in cases of doubt about any facts of those rules, resource consumption will prevail.*[71]

Ironically, our legal system sanctions environmental lawlessness. The failure to recognize the right to *freedom from* consumption abrogates the group rights of environmentalists, which are already in jeopardy in the legal system.

Environmental dissidents are marginalized because a technocratic consumer society atomizes the concept of pluralism. Pluralism can refer only to individualism within the internal variety of the market, never to groups at variance from the market. A consumer society subsumes the meanings of pluralism and individuality to the logic of the market economy, much as a Marxist economy subsumes their meanings to the logic of the state. The cultural pluralism of a group presents a category alien to the technological mindset. Just as the concept of biodiversity is inimical to the industry's technological approach to the forest, so too is cultural pluralism anathema to society's concept of itself as a monoculture. Pluralism comes to be interpreted within a narrow view of individualism, just as words such as "diversity," "selective" and "sustainable" come to have meanings in industry adapted to abusive ends.[72]

In a consumer society, the individual is the person who is free because s/he has acquisitive power. The unemployed has no individuality, s/he is faceless because s/he has no power to consume. A cultural group that steps out of the consumer role is not readily identifiable, and therefore is presumed not to exist. Indeed, the idea of rejecting the consumer relationship is inconceivable from the logic of mainstream society. The group character of dissidents presents a challenge that technocratic consumer society cannot absorb without relinquishing its hegemony. As Ronald Garet states:

> ...the crucial thing to keep in mind is the scheme of individual and social values as the grounds for rights and governmental authority.... It is this scheme that ultimately supplies the jurisprudence of constitutional rights with a double argument for the view that those rights must be individual rights, not group rights.... Rights are concerns for individuals and for society rather than for groups. The more negative side of the argument shows how the individual and social values account for governmental power to regulate and control groups. *Thus groups are doubly vulnerable;* they are especially important targets of governmental regulation and they are conspicuously missing from the coverage of fundamental rights.[73]

By approaching the problem of rights exclusively from the perspective of individual and societal rights, the ground for group rights is tacitly overlooked, as the Clayoquot defendants were to discover.

In the Clayoquot trials the decision to criminalize civil contempt was an abuse of societal rights in favour of the rights of the corporate individual, MacMillan Bloedel. As we saw in the use of the map of TFL 44, the courts assumed that MacMillan Bloedel was the voice of society, because it was upheld by the government. In ordering the criminalization of the injunction, the Attorney General exercised a political and legal advantage over environmentalists, by exploiting their vulnerability as a cultural group. His was a political decision to regulate a distinct social group, by overlooking its group rights. In so doing, the government excluded a substantial number of people from a legitimate expression of group rights consistent with the fundamental rights of individuals. Their cultural expectations, like those of First Nations, came from a distinct ontological view of humanity which legitimized their democratic opposition to a global ideology based on cultural rape.

## Conclusion

Although the debate on Clayoquot Sound has been focussed on the social and environmental problems posed by clearcutting, the heart of the question lies far deeper. What we witness in phenomena like Mardola Falls, Redwood Summer, and Clayoquot Sound, is a need for a reassessment of our cultural direction. The problem that Clayoquot Sound posed to the government and to the courts was an ontological one. It asked something we are rarely given the time to reflect upon in the information bombardment of technocratic-industrial society: what it means to be human.

Western philosophers such as John Locke, who provided the political theory that gave rise to our constitution and the human rights tradition, have given some guidance on this matter. For

Locke, an essential human quality is the ability to identify with other species. The ability of humans to recognize their responsibilities to other beings is essential because those

> who delight in the suffering of inferior creatures, will not...be very compassionate or benign to those of their own kind.[74]

Our sense of identity with others gave rise to the Anglo-American liberal tradition which produced our modern sense of rights. Even from the scant knowledge that seventeenth-century science had of nature, Locke seems to have intuited a greater sense of affinity and responsibility to nature than contemporary industrial society allows our humanity. The limited biological knowledge we have today, if only of our genetic proximity to so many of the life-forms with whom we share this planet, should enhance that dimension of our identity.

The realization of the human link to nature is a keystone in the democratic tradition. Subservience to technology stems from the assumption that to be human is to be distinct, somehow superior to all other life-forms. It introduces a line of superiorist and anti-democratic thought. The belief in humanity's exclusivity is a cultural choice. Regrettably, this belief in our uniqueness gains ever more credence as human beings isolate themselves from the direct experience of nature and other cultures. Contemporary industrial life in all its forms aims for a "virtual reality" on an "information highway"—an overload of disinformation that distorts reality. If a culture is a sign system that produces meaning, then technological culture with its capacity to divorce humans from an experiential connection may well be the first non-culture, for connection is the source of meaning.

Although nature has always been part of our identity since the dawn of time, technology divorces us from that identity. Some may dream of artificial environments as improvements on nature, but the scientific and social fiasco of mega-million dollar projects like Biosphere II tells us about our real condition, and brings us back to earth.

The Clayoquot protest is about the necessity to come to terms with the reality of the human condition. The social failure to take into account the human and cultural dimensions of Clayoquot offers a key to understanding why the external or political problems it posed may have no adequate resolution in the near future. Not until we reassess our conception of our relation to nature, instead of thinking of better means to exploit what little remains of nature, will we find a solution.

In the Clayoquot trials the courts' lack of appreciation of the human and cultural dimension of the aspirations of the environmental protestors revealed how difficult it is to gain public acceptance of the need to re-assess our contract with nature. Throughout the trials, it was shocking to note that, while group rights were trampled by courts and governments, and individuals were being tried on matters of conscience, none of the associations concerned with abuses of law made a single compassionate move. Amnesty International was silent and The Canadian Civil Liberties Association found the Clayoquot trials acceptable. Had the accused been a readily recognizable social group, such associations would undoubtedly have risen to protect the protestors. What distinguished this case from others supported by these associations was that the protestors held ecocentric cultural beliefs that the anthropocentric majority of our urban globalized society could not understand without putting into question its own beliefs.

In this respect, it is important to note that the courts were limited by a structural problem of legal policy. The courts are instruments of societal values. Blame should not be deflected exclusively onto the courts, when the problem was endemic in society. The problem lay in a collective amnesia: the majority chose not to look, question or try to understand. The Attorney General, the government and the industry took advantage of a weakness in the legal system in order to misuse the law to a political end, but this was only possible through the silent approbation of the majority. Clayoquot could be dismissed when the media presented it by focussing on key figures as another contention between pro- and anti-logging. A truly critical point of view would have revealed the affinity of this protest with countless others created by ordinary people attempting to recover a sense of connection to those things that have always provided humanity with cultural meaningfulness. In the end, we can see that Clayoquot was an extra-ordinary affirmation of seemingly ordinary people asserting their rights against the pervasive practice of cultural rape.

### Notes

1. For an analysis of the breakdown and crisis of the North-American social condition, see Arthur Croker and David Cook, *The Postmodern Scene,* Montreal: 1983, and Frances Moore Lappé, *Rediscovering America's Values,* New York: 1989.

2. Neil Postman, quoted in Maria Bohulawsky, "Culture Rape, a brain drain on '90's youth," *Vancouver Sun,* June 17, 1994. The contents of the lecture Postman gave in Ottawa seem to sum up his excellent book: *Technopoly: The Surrender of Culture to Technology,* New York: 1992.

3. Although "culture" is a controversial concept in the social sciences, the fact that discussion is impossible without referring to the existence of cultural phenomena has led to an acceptance of its relational character. See Diane Austin-Broos (ed.), *Creating Culture,* Allen and Unwin, 1987.

4. Abraham Maslow, "Synergy in the Society and in the Individual," *The Farther Reaches of Human Nature,* Penguin: 1971, 191-202.

5. For a theoretical survey of these problems, see Stephen R. Kellert and E. O. Wilson, *The Biophilia Hypothesis,* Island Press: 1993. An anthropological approach can be found in R.M. Netting, *Cultural Ecology,* Waveland Press: 1986. The basis for a jurisprudential approach can be found in Gisday Wa and Delgam Uukw, *The Spirit in The Land,* Gabriola: 1989.

6. For the implications of the drive to monoculture, see John Rodman, "The Liberation of Nature?" *Inquiry,* 20, 1977, 83-145.

7. Chris Manes, *Green Rage: Radical Environmentalism and the Unmaking of Civilization,* Boston: 1990; and R. Scarce, *Eco-Warriors: Understanding the Radical Environmental Movement,* Chicago: 1990.

8. For the study of maps and their sociological implications, see Peter Jackson, *Maps of Meaning: An introduction to cultural geography,* London: 1989.

9. By the end of the summer some 930 were arrested, over 860 were charged with criminal contempt.

10. The meaning of places for First Nations and environmentalists transcends racial and cultural boundaries, as can be seen in the statement of the American Indian Movement leader, Russell Means, "Fighting Words for The Future of The Earth," *Mother Jones,* December 1980, 24-38.

11. On the adverse impacts of industrial agriculture, see Lester Brown, "Feeding Six Billion," *The World Watch Reader on Environmental Issues,* Norton: 1991: 147-164; Alan Thein Durling, "Supporting Indigenous Peoples," *State of*

*the World: 1993*; for a realistic assessment of the implications of industrial agriculture on the destruction of North-American life and values, Wendell Berry, *The Unsettling of America*, Sierra Club: 1977; and W. Berry, W. Jackson and B. Colman, *Meeting The Expectations of The Land*, North Point: 1983.

12. Quoted from, Daniel Francis, *The Imaginary Indian*, Vancouver: Arsenal, 1992, p. 200.

13. Statistics Canada revealed that approximately 66% of First Nations people have had the privilege of residing in our prisons. When numbers reach this proportion it is not indicative of the criminality of the residents, but of the criminality of the society that marginalizes its members.

14. This key concept and its implications were made clear by the report on the essence of Zuni culture by the nineteenth-century anthropologist, Frank Cushing, "Zuni Fetiches," *Zuni: Selected Writings*, University of Nebraska: 1979, 194-204. The universality of this concept among First Nations has been evinced by the cosmological work on Mayan culture, David Freidel, Linda Schele and Joy Parker, *Mayan Cosmos*, New York: 1993.

15. See Hugh Brody among the Dunne-Za, *Maps and Dreams*, Douglas and McIntyre, 1981.

16. P. Tennant, *Aboriginal Peoples and Politics*, UBC: 1990, and *Aboriginal Appeals* vols I-II, Court of Appeal For British Columbia, CA 013770, 1993.

17. This reasoning applies not only to land, but to slaves. The famous example is the hanging of the slave girls who had consorted with the suitors in the house of Odysseus. Their execution is simply a form of house cleaning that reasserts the control of the master.

18. The term used here is "aboriginal" as distinct from First Nations, because of the jurisprudential history of this problem. "Aboriginal" is used to refer to all cultures that existed throughout the world (Maori, Aborigenes, Zulu etc.) whose land claims have been the object of Anglo-American jurisprudence. "First Nations" refers to the nations that have occupied the North American land mass since contact.

19. See Lambert J., in *Aboriginal Appeals*, vol. 1, 150, 164.

20. Lambert, 169.

21. See Lambert, 211-220.

22. The commonly held misperception is that First Nation culture must somehow remain frozen in time to retain its authenticity. Part of the "authenticity" is a conformity to the "material basis of culture." Regrettably for the Marxist beliefs of social scientists, cultures evolve internally and adapt their perceptions to material artefacts: they are therefore not determined by material conditions, but by the manner in which they interpret them. The falsehood that lies in the veiled racism of the view that "Indians" have lost their "authenticity" has been ably addressed by Daniel Francis, The *Imaginary Indian*, Arsenal: 1992.

Clayoquot: Recovering from Cultural Rape

23. The cultural separation of humans from nature is normally referred to as the eco-wall. The monocultural negation of the existence of other cultures is simply an extension of the same wall. See Scarce, *Eco-Warriors*, 7-29.

24. Lambert, 244.

25. See Rodman, "The Rights of Nature," (supra); Christopher Stone, *Should Trees Have Standing?*, Los Altos (California): Kaufmann, 1972; and "Should Trees Have Standing? Revisited," *Southern California Law Review*, vol. 59, no. 1, 1-154; and Roderick Nash, *The Rights of Nature*, Wisconsin: 1989.

26. Rudolph C. Ryser, "Nation States, Indigenous Nations, and The Great Lie," in Leroy Little Bear, Menno Boldt and J.A. Long (eds.), *Pathways To Self-Determination*, Toronto: 1984.

27. See A. Gore, "Dysfunctional Civilization," *Earth in Balance*, Boston: 1992, pp. 216-237.

28. Gottfried Dietze, *Magna Carta and Property*, Charlottesville: 1965.

29. For a survey of the evolution of First Nations' empowerment, see Roger Moody (ed.), *The Indigenous Voice: Visions and Realities*, Utrecht: 1993, Part iv: Conscientisation and Recovery of Origins, Chapter 5: "The New Indians," pp. 466-476. The evolution of the Radical Environmental Movement has been the object of two recent studies: Victor B. Scheffer, *The Shaping of Environmentalism in America*, University of Washington: 1991; and Philip Shabecoff, *A Fierce Green Fire*, Hill and Wang: 1993.

30. The communality of interests, which was well documented at Clayoquot, can be seen in the importance of environmental impact on First Nations (*Indigenous Voices* Part 3: "Present Struggles," pp. 130-243; John H. Bodley, *Victims of Progress*, Mayfield: 1990 pp. 147-150).

31. See Charlene Spretnak and Fritjof Capra, *Green Politics*, New Mexico: Bear and Co., 1986.

32. On the ideology and effects of the Scientific Revolution in the shaping of European sensitivity to nature, see Carolyn Merchant, *The Death of Nature*, New York: Harper & Row, 1980. On the consequences of the Industrial revolution, see Clive Ponting, *A Green History of the World*, London, 1991; and I.G. Simmons, *Environmental History*, Oxford: Blackwell, 1993, pp. 29-47.

33. The social implications of holistic and prescriptive technology has been studied by Ursula Franklin, *The Real World of Technology*, CBC Enterprises: 1990. As an ex-professor of engineering, Franklin rightly notes the illusory character of the freedom promised by technology: "often the promise of liberation in the first stages of the introduction of a technology is not subsequently fulfilled, and there is quite a sophisticated mechanism of building up dependency after..." (pp. 118-119).

34. It has become common practice to revile the Bible and Judeo-Christianity for the Western alienation from the land. The argument was initiated by Lynn

193

White Jr. "The Historical Roots of Our Ecologic Crisis," *Science*, 155: 1203-1207, 1967; and Frederick Turner, *The Western Spirit Against Wilderness*, Rutgers: 1980. White's position was not clearly defined in the 1967 paper, as discussed by Nash, *The Rights of Nature*, pp. 90-96. The problems posed by this view of the Biblical narratives are various. They lead to a confusion regarding the flexibility of the text and the rigidity of the dominant interpretations of the institutions. A further problem is that it gives rise to anti-semitic associations. In the first place, both Judaism and Christianity are characterized by a proliferation of heterodox currents, that (as in the case of deep ecology) have always belonged to a minority and recurrent ecocentric tradition. This begins of course with Judaism's own roots in the cult to the goddess. See Raphael Patai, *The Hebrew Goddess*, New York: 1991.

35. Donald Worster, *Nature's Economy*, Cambridge: 1977.

36. Frederic Clements, *Dynamics of Vegetation*, New York: 1949; "Social Origins and Processes among Plants," *A Handbook of Social Psychology* (ed.) C. Murchison, Worcester Mass: 1935.

37. Aldo Leopold, "The Land Ethic," *A Sand County Almanac*, Oxford: (1949), repr. 1989. Although prepared for publication in 1948, "The Land Ethic" was really first formulated in 1939 by Leopold in "A Biotic View of The Land," published in *The Journal of Forestry*. See Aldo Leopold, *The River of The Mother of God And Other Essays*, (eds.) Susan Flader and J. Baird Callicott, Madison: 1991.

38. J.E. Lovelock, *A New Look At Life On Earth*, Oxford: 1979, and Stephen H. Schneider and P.J. Boston, *Scientists on Gaia*, Cambridge, Mass: 1991.

39. Roderick Nash, *Wilderness and the American Mind*, 3rd ed. Yale: (1967), repr. 1982.

40. *The Rights of Nature*, 12.

41. See Franklin, *The Real World of Technology*; as well as L. Mumford, *The Myth of the Machine* and *The Pentagon of Power*, vols. 1-2 New York: 1966-7; Herbert Marcuse, *One Dimensional Man*, Boston: 1964; Jacques Ellul, *The Technological Society*, New York, 1964; K. Popper, *The Open Society and Its Enemies*, vols. 1-2, Princeton: 1962.

42. For an insight into the subservience of science as a technology in service of political ideologies, see David Suzuki, "Genetics After Auschwitz," *Inventing the Future: Reflections on Science, Technology and Nature*, Toronto: 1989, 24-40.

43. T.S. Kuhn, *The Structure of Scientific Revolutions*, Chicago: 1970; and Karl Popper, *The Logic of Scientific Discovery*, New York: 1968.

44. Karl Popper, "The Problem of Demarcation (1974)," *Popper Selections*, (ed.) David Miller, Princeton: 1985, 118-132.

45. For a first-hand survey of this unhealthy relationship between 1930 and 1970, and the degree to which the Faculty of Forestry has failed in its public responsibility, see Ian Mahood and Ken Drushka, *Three Men and A Forester*,

Harbour: 1990, especially page 44.

46. Frances Foran, "Conflict of Interest at UBC," *The Ubyssey* vol. 75, no. 12, October 20, 1992.

47. "Conflict of Interest at UBC."

48. In November 1993, having realized the extent to which its decision had been discredited, the government created the "Scientific Panel for Sustainable Forest Practices in Clayoquot Sound." This governmental and corporate use of science is again deceitful. Although the panel is peopled by numerous scientists of merit, its mandate is not to review the decision, but to review the most appropriate extraction methods in an irreversible decision. See T*he Scientific Panel for Sustainable Forest Practices in Clayoquot Sound,* Progress Report 2: *Review of Current Forest Practice Standards in Clayoquot Sound.* May 10, 1994, page 4, section 1.1.

49. These beliefs are largely associated with the corporate practice of disinformation through the SHARE groups, as detailed in Donald Snow, "Wise Use and Public Lands in The West," *Utne Reader,* no. 63, May/June 1994, 70-82. This tendentious type of publicity was also found in *The Vancouver Sun.* See Thomas Wright, "A Plea for Old Forestry," 12 February 1994; Denny Boyd, "Swede Saw Massacre of Island," March 25, 1994; Gordon Hamilton, "NDP Native Forestry Condemned," April 28, 1994; or Cheng C. Ying, "Man-made Forests Hold The Key," *The Victoria Times-Colonist,* January 25, 1994.

50. Technology then appears, as Mumford suggests, as an evolution of the ability of humans to stabilize the food supply and increase the size of local populations, which develops into the basis of imperialist ideology, as argued by Alfred W. Cosby, *Ecological Imperialisms: The Biological Expansion of Europe, 900-1900,* Cambridge: 1986.

51. Wendell Berry, "The Ecological Crisis as a Crisis of Character," *The Unsettling of America,* pp. 17-27.

52. The influence of Burson-Marsteller and its interference in everything from freedom of the press to community structure has been amply documented in Kim Goldberg, "Axed," *This Magazine,* August 1993, 11-15; Joyce Nelson, "Burson-Marsteller, Pax Trilateral and the Brundtland Gang vs. the Environment," *The New Catalyst,* Summer 1993; "Pulp and Propaganda," *Canadian Forum* July/August 1994, 15-19.

53. This phenomenon is well explained by Chris Manes, "The Rise and Fall of Reform Environmentalism: An Unexpurgated History," *Green Rage,* pp. 45-65.

54. Phrase used by Justice Bouck in his judgement of the first 44 protestors.

55. Andrew MacLaughlin, "The Critique of Humanity and Nature," *The Trumpeter,* vol. 4, n. 4, 1987, p. 2.

56. Arne Naess, "The Shallow and the Deep, Long-Range Ecology Movements," *Inquiry* 16, 1974, pp. 95-100; *Ecology, Community and Lifestyle,* (trans.) David Rothenberg, Cambridge: 1989.

57. Arne Naess, _Ecology, Community and Lifestyle,_ pp. 47-65.

58. See Arne Naess, _Gandhi and Group Conflict,_ Oslo: 1974, and "Non-violence and The Philosophy of Oneness," _Ecology Community and Lifestyle,_ pp. 193-196. As well as Huxley's defense of satyagraha in an age of technology, _Science Liberty and Peace,_ London: 1946.

59. "Charter of Rights and Freedoms: Fundamental Freedoms," _Current Issue Review,_ 84-16E, Library of Parliament: Research Branch, May 14, 1982, p. 3.

60. _Current Issue Review,_ p. 2.

61. C. H. MacIlwain, "Magna Carta and Common Law," _Magna Carta Commemoration Essays,_ (ed.) H.E. Malden, London: 1917, pp. 122-179.

62. Re W (1971) A.C. 682, p. 700. See also the ample discussion of this problem, in André Morel, "La clause limitative de l'article 1 de la Charte Canadienne," _The Canadian Bar Review,_ vol. 61, March 1983, pp. 81-100.

63. That is the gist of the ruling of Dickson J., in _Perka et al. v The Queen_ 13 _D.L.R._(1984), pp. 6-28, which governed all subsequent rulings on the types of defenses possible in a case of criminal contempt.

64. H. W. Pettigrew, "A Constitutional Right of Freedom From Ecocide," _Environmental Law,_ 1971, pp. 1-2.

65. See _Green Rage,_ pp. 204-205.

66. Mark MacGuigan, "Democracy and Civil Disobedience," _Canadian Bar Review,_ XLIX, 1971, p. 255.

67. D.W. Large and P. Michie, "Proving That The Strength Of The British Navy Depends On The Number of Old Maids In England: A Comparison of Scientific With Legal Proof," _Environmental Law,_ vol. 11, 1981, pp. 596-597.

68. To appreciate the extent to which the doctrine of proximate cause is out of touch with the dangers posed by the power of technology to destroy life on earth, and the resultant need to base decisions on the basis of caution, see Hans Jonas, _The Imperative of Responsibility: In Search of An Ethics for the Technological Age,_ Chicago: 1988.

69. 3 _W.W.R._ 481 (S.C.C.) p. 493.

70. Ronald Garet, "Communality and Existence: The Rights of Groups," _Southern California Law Review,_ 56, 1983, p. 1002.

71. Krier, "Environmental Litigation and Burden of Proof," in Large and Michie "Proving That The Strength Of The British Navy," p. 608.

72. On the use of these words, see Reed F. Noss, "A Sustainable Forest is a Diverse and Sustainable Forest," _Clearcut: The Tragedy of Industrial Forestry,_ pp. 33-38.

73. Ron Garet, _SCLR,_ 56, 1983, p. 1012.

74. John Locke, _Some Thoughts on Education_ (1693).

# The Clayoquot Protests:
# Taking Stock One Year Later

CHRISTOPHER HATCH

*"...I've told you a hundred different times—that there is nothing wrong with the world. What's wrong is our way of looking at it."*
— Henry Miller

*"Nature Bats Last"*
— bumpersticker

Did the Clayoquot protests fail? That question haunts us as the clearcutting continues its juggernaut of greed through the ancient rainforests of Clayoquot Sound. All those people roused from slumber on our communal train to annihilation. Twelve thousand people protesting at a remote bridge, standing up for a forest most had never seen. Over 900 hauled away by the police. Hundreds more arrested outside Canadian embassies overseas. Rallies and protests around the globe. It was so much more than anyone could have expected, so much more than anything Canadians had ever seen. It was so strong, so powerful, so un-Canadian in its determination. The quiet, fragile power of conscience protecting the remnants of the natural world from our culture's drunken orgy of destruction.

But the clearcuts continue to tear through the fjords of Clayoquot Sound. After decades of peaceful struggle, the Escalante region is barren, the Atleo watershed stripped, the Cypre denuded. Streams are silted, creeks forced underground, salmon are disappearing. And yet the clearcutting goes on. Political leaders locked into debates the rest of us stopped listening to ages ago. Industrial leaders too myopic to read writing on a wall that we are fast approaching.

The frustration above all is that everyone agrees we are in deep shit. Anyone with a few drinks in them will admit that homo sapiens are on the verge of committing communal suicide. But we're just not very good at making the connections between the obvious general problem and its specific manifestations when they occur in our own backyards. Canadians sat twirling acid rain-drenched skeletons of maple leaves while the Atlantic fishing industry collapsed. Our fossil-fuel frenzied neighbours can no longer fish for salmon off the American West Coast. We have torn holes in the sky over our heads and poisoned our oceans and lakes. Every day 40 to 100 species disappear forever into an extinction crisis too frightening even to contemplate. And as a final farcical icing on a very ill-tasting cake, we stand a very real chance of turning our planet into a giant unsurvivable sauna.

*And Clayoquot Sound is still being clearcut.*

So were the protests futile? The outlook is pretty bleak if they were. It's hard to see what more could have been done. Civil disobedience is the strongest stand a citizen can make. The strongest message we can send to powerholders, the hardest kick in the butt we can each, individually, give our society. And the kick is well placed. Our treatment of the forests of British Columbia is where we might start doing our bit to steer away from the cliff we appear to be intent on driving over. Forests are home to three-quarters of the world's species. Half to three-quarters of the world's natural forests have already been eliminated. As far as temperate rainforests go, there never was much. Just a thin thread of forest caught between towering mountain ranges and crashing oceans and squeezed along a few western coastlines.

Less than one percent of the planet to start with. Huge, ancient, fine-grained trees. Unfortunately for them, ideal for timber and other wood products. More than half of them are gone. The only big chunks left are in B.C., Alaska and Chile. That's it. Half of all that's left is in North America, over half of that is in British Columbia.[1]

Our politicos tell us they've heard the message. Massaging their bruised hinds they spew rhetoric about new directions for forestry. "World class logging" and "performance based logging" have become the jargon of the day.

We've heard all this before of course but, just to be fair, Greenpeace commissioned a random audit of recent and active clearcuts in the Clayoquot Sound region. It was released in July of 1994. The results? Every single cutblock in violation of even the "old" standards. Between sixty and one hundred violations in all. Damage to salmon streams, eroding topsoil, logging outside designated boundaries and landslides are still business as usual.[2]

These results confirm government-commissioned audits carried out across the province in 1992 and 1994. Those studies, popularly known as the "Tripp reports" after their author, showed that more than one stream with "fisheries concerns" gets damaged per clearcut.[3]

And even with all the attention and all the controversy and all the promises, there is still only one single method of logging being used in Clayoquot Sound—Clearcutting.

*Rhetoric aside, very little has changed on the ground.*

In the broader context we have seen some change. Some of it progressive and some not. The provincial government, intent on wiping some egg off its face before the next election, has produced a series of initiatives designed to placate its upstart citizenry. The federal government's Committee on Natural Resources has held a series of hearings on the joys of clearcutting. The major logging companies, faced with a marketplace eager to appear green, have turned several shades of green themselves as they come to terms with the increasingly precarious future for their bottom line. Ecoforestry and selection logging institutes and woodlot operators are enjoying an all-time high.

Billions of dollars worth of the European pulp and paper market is now committed to buying clearcut-free products. Two major British companies have cancelled contracts with Macmillan Bloedel because of its logging in Clayoquot Sound. *The New York Times* has refused to buy pulp or paper from Clayoquot Sound. And those are just the big shots.

If anything proves that the Clayoquot and similar protests have been influential, it is the response from government and industry. A sophisticated series of television, newspaper and radio advertisements has been launched to convince the public that all is well in the woods. A multi-million-dollar overseas campaign, paid for in tax dollars, is being waged to convince importers that any problems in British Columbia's forests have been solved. A recent report in *Canadian Forum* tallies the total cost of the anti-environmental push at $46.8 million over the next five years. The P.R. firm involved, Burson Marsteller, has achieved infamy for its involvement in damage control with the likes of Union Carbide during the Bhopal disaster, and Exxon during the Exxon Valdez oil spill.[4]

The provincial government's initiatives and plans are probably the least easy to get your head around. Two positive developments have begun in Clayoquot Sound. Both have implications much further afield. Picking up on the two prongs of the campaign to protect Clayoquot Sound—land rights for First Nations and ecological integrity for the region—the province has signed an accord with the Nuu-chah-nulth and has set up a panel of scientific experts to review industrial activities in Clayoquot.

The agreement with the central region tribes of the Nuu-chah-nulth has been touted variously as "the end to colonialism"[5] or a sleazy way to take the wind out of environmental sails. Government intentions aside, the Nuu-chah-nulth tribal council feel they have negotiated a promising beginning to recovering control of their traditional lands. Non-native environmentalists disagree over how substantive the agreement really is, but have decided for the most part to keep their mouths shut. Telling First Nations people what is good for them is colonialism as surely as is logging off their lands without permission. Viewed in this light, the

Clayoquot protesters have been successful in one out of their two demands. The Nuu-chah-nulth have a say in the management of their lands.

I wish the Nuu-chah-nulth well. Their lands sure aren't in the same shape as when they were stolen.

The second government initiative in Clayoquot is a promising combination of high-powered scientists and highly respected Native people. The Clayoquot Sound Science Panel has delivered two reports, both of which blend traditional ways of knowing with scientific understandings of conservation biology. So far, so good. Their final recommendations have not yet been released but, without a doubt, we will be better off than we are at present. Any chink in the "clearcuts or bust" armour of the companies will be invaluable.

The government initiatives that are not specific to Clayoquot Sound hold less promise. Some are a blatant leap backwards. None stands up well in comparison to progress that has already been made in other countries. Everyone agrees that a "Forest Practices Code" is a long overdue piece of legislation. The content of the one we have been given, however, is a matter for disagreement. The spin doctors are spouting "stricter rules" and "tougher enforcement." More level heads have pointed out that its primary contribution is to make clearcutting the legally enshrined logging method of choice. As far as "world class logging" goes, just be glad you're not a British Columbian salmon. The Code provides less protection for salmon spawning streams in B.C. than the United States accords streams without fish. The Code also develops new tenets in ecological theory. Most notable is that anyone following an "operational plan" cannot, by definition, cause "environmental damage."[6] Who knew there were still legislator-philosophers?

Another initiative, the "Forest Renewal Plan," is being hailed as the Camp David accord of the old-growth wars. But a little caution might be in order when logging companies are happy about someone doubling the prices they pay to cut public forests. Perhaps all the stuff about intensifying the conversion of B.C.'s forests into tree farms caused a smile or two in the odd boardroom?

The "Vancouver Island Land Use Plan" is not as popular among CEO's. It is the government's version of the CORE (Commission on Resources and the Environment) proposal combined with the Brundtland Commission's magical 12 percent protection goal. Under the plan, protected areas increase to account for about 13 percent of the Island's land area. Any self-respecting tree hugger has to be happy about the protection of long fought-over areas in the Walbran and Carmanah watersheds. Cynical voices among them note that the struggle lasted so long that the number of trees left to hug in those areas has been greatly diminished. Other cynics note that the 13 percent includes a disproportionately high percentage of the Island's alpine and glaciated regions, while only about seven percent of the rainforest is offlimits to chainsaws.

The CORE process is one very encouraging development. A sharp change from the status quo of closed doors and backroom deals, the CORE process sits everyone down at the same table to hash out their differences and come to some agreement. No surprise that it didn't work. The group did not reach consensus, but it was promising that the government even tried. The next obvious step is for everyone to agree that the biological realities of life are not one among the many "interest groups" at the table. But one thing at a time.

It is really in the wider, societal context that the Clayoquot protests can claim to be successful. Environmental concerns have been catapulted to an entirely new level on political agendas. If ever blind exploitation of the natural world takes its proper place in the annals of historic barbarisms, it may be that the Clayoquot protests will be seen as the turning point in Canadian history. The point at which mainstream society decided our captain needed radically new sailing orders. The point at which we realized that jail was pretty cushy compared to where we were heading: at best a thoroughly homogenized globe but even more likely some Mad Max vision of ecological collapse.

One distinct change that has spun out of the summer of 1993 is that our society is no longer just arguing about parks. Earlier, the primary question had been whether to protect five percent or twelve percent or even twenty percent, now we are asking what should be done with the other eighty or ninety percent. What kind of place do we want to live in anyway? Should a practice like clearcutting be allowed anywhere? It's a fundamentally important dimension to the debate. It's about learning to live in the world instead of off the world. It's about learning to be friendly to our neighbours regardless of gender, race, or species. It's about learning to take responsibility for our own mess.

Clearcutting ranks with strip mining and driftnetting as some of the most destructive industrial practices ever devised. With absolutely no consideration to taking only what we want, let alone only how much we need, we attack vast tracts of forest, killing everything in a furious grab for certain species of tree. No thought given to how much we have to leave behind for the forest to be able to survive. No thought given to how we might remove certain trees without levelling an entire ecosystem. Barbarism, pure and simple.

*Ninety percent of the logging in Canada is clearcutting. Almost one hundred percent along the Pacific coast.*[7]

Clearcutting is now a hot issue. Since the summer of 1993, we have this particular bull firmly by the horns. It's only to be expected that it will bellow and charge and trample a good many thousands of acres before it stops to catch its breath and take a clear look around. Of course, there is no guarantee that the bull won't break free. This one, especially, is louder and more testosterone-filled than most of us had realized. We all have a lot of work before us.

It is work that has got to be done. Clearcuts are chomping voraciously into our forests. And let's not kid ourselves, clearcutting is deforestation. Trees may grow back but a forest won't. Not in our lifetimes, and maybe never.

Cross your fingers, but things seem to be starting to change. Although you would be forgiven for not having noticed the signs of change over the companies' high decibel screams of outrage. The industry claims everything from rural communities to urban hospitals will collapse if their divine right to clearcut is questioned. Clearcutting, we are told, is the only possible way to log. But people seem to be starting to remember that, in the past, when cutting down a tree meant a lot more work, leaving the ones you didn't need seemed very possible indeed.

Woodlot owners have been arguing for years that it is actually more productive over the long run to cut and remove individual trees at a rate not exceeding the growth rate of a forest. It's just common sense really, and scientists as well as politicians are beginning to get the picture. For months, public forests in Washington, Oregon and Northern California have been tied up in the courts because of proven destruction wrought by clearcut logging on those ecosystems. The crisis is so advanced that the Pacific Northwestern United States has only 10 to 15 percent of its old-growth left. The American government is now going to allow companies back into some public forests, but they will have to leave some of the forest's structure behind when they leave. It's only modified clearcutting really, but it's a step in the right direction. The scientists recognized the unnaturalness and outright destructiveness of clearcutting, and the politicians realized that the better you treat the land, the less of it the public will demand in parks. And the companies? Well, everyone realized that the companies can be told to do whatever needs to be done and they'll do it. And they'll make a profit at it.

"It took a century and a half to arrive at the current crisis in the Pacific Northwest," according to U.S. Federal government scientists.[8] Up here, north of the 49th parallel, we have more of our natural forests left. Conventional wisdom has it that we are a couple of decades "behind" the Pacific Northwest, and we still have the chance to learn from their experience before our forests are as fragmented and degraded as theirs. As yet, we see little movement from our politicians to address the problems of clearcutting, but companies, spurred on by the situation of their American affiliates, are beginning to investigate "alternative silviculture systems." They won't give up clearcutting until they're forced to, but they seem to be preparing for that day.

Canadian scientists are now addressing the problems of clearcutting head on. Environment Canada's 1994 report on "Biodiversity in British Columbia" states unequivocally that clearcutting causes a "loss in biodiversity" and warns that this may have "economic and social, as well as ecological repercussions." The Federal government scientists go on to say that "Modern methods of partial cutting can be selected and designed to maintain the structural attributes of old-growth forest, wildlife habitat, or other non-timber values. However...about 90% of the harvested forests...are clear-cut."[9]

The Clayoquot Sound Science Panel has already recommended a shift to "ecosystem management," the buzzword of the recent American developments, as well as an avoidance of the practice of clearcutting.[10]

So there are signs of hope out there. And we can credit the Clayoquot protests with having served notice that people are beginning to recognize the gravity of our situation, and that politicians are going to be expected to take care of things from now on. "Stop the world, we want to get off" was the awakening joke of the sixties. "Slow it down, we'd better think about this" was the reasoned plea of the Clayoquot jailbirds. Whether or not it happened in time, and whether or not the brakes are applied hard enough, the Clayoquot protestors have had their voices heard.

We can only hope that the Clayoquot protests turn out to have been a watershed in our society's evolution towards balance and responsibility, not merely an early spasm in the death throes of a society pathologically bent on destroying its environs and obsessed with consuming itself. More than a brief moment of lucidity in a maelstrom of psychosis.

> *"It's like our society is heading towards the edge of a cliff. We're either going to fall over it or we're going to learn to fly."*
> — Rya Shankman, age 15. Speaking to sentence in the Supreme Court of British Columbia.

Notes

1. Ecotrust and Conservation International, 1992. *Coastal Temperate Rain Forests: Ecological Characteristics, Status and Distribution Worldwide.*

2. Sierra Legal Defense Fund, 1994. *An Independent Environmental Assessment of Active and Recent Cutblocks in Clayoquot Sound and the Port Alberni Forest District.* Prepared for Greenpeace Canada.

3. D. Tripp, 1994. *The Use and Effectiveness of the Coastal Fisheries Forestry Guidelines in Selected Forest Districts of Coastal British Columbia.* Ministry of Forests, Integrated Resources Branch.

4. Joyce Nelson, "Pulp and Propaganda," in *The Canadian Forum.* July/Aug, 1994.

5. B.C. Premier Michael Harcourt, Speech: University of Hamburg. January, 1994.

6. Legislative Assembly of British Columbia, 1994. *Bill 40, Forest Practices Code of British Columbia Act.*

7. Forestry Canada, 1994. *The State of Canada's Forests* 1993.

8. Forest Ecosystem Management Team, 1993. *Forest Ecosystem Management: An Ecological, Economic, and Social Assessment.* United States Departments of: Agriculture, Commerce, Interior; and the Environmental Protection Agency.

9. L. Harding and E. McCullum, eds., 1994. *Biodiversity in British Columbia.* Environment Canada.

10. Clayoquot Sound Scientific Panel, 1994. *Report #2.*

# Clayoquot Sound, 1994: Ongoing Industrial Logging Violations

*The unsustainable, unacceptable forest practices of past decades must never be used again.*
—Premier Harcourt, news release from the office of the Premier,
November 9, 1993

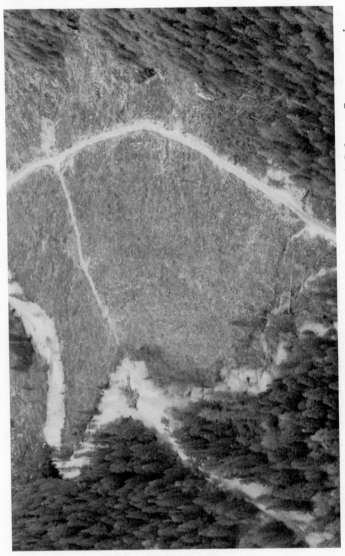

Tofino Creek, March 1994. Regulations for this size of Class A Salmon Stream require a "leave strip" of 30 Metres along the riparian zone.

Atleo River, March 1994.

Cold Creek, July 1994. Road erosion due to improper drainage control and lack of road maintenance. Silt flows into salmon-spawning grounds below.

Bawden Creek tributary, Class A salmon stream. May 1994. Clearcut winter of 1992/3. Shows logging to edge (regulations require 20 metre "leave strip"), with degradation of stream banks by erosion and operation of heavy equipment. Water no longer flows in this channel.

Cypre River, May 1994. Recent clearcut from mountain top to river's edge.

Cypre River, May 1994. New road and bridge. Note debris and cat tracks in river bed. TFL 44 harvested by MB.

*Tzeporah Berman* was a blockade coordinator and spokesperson for the Friends of Clayoquot Sound in the summer of 1993. In an attempt to quell public dissent, the RCMP arrested her on July 16, 1993, off the side of the road, allegedly for "aiding and abetting" those who chose to be arrested on the blockades. One year later the case was thrown out of court. For the past year she has worked as a forests campaigner for Greenpeace Canada and is currently finishing her Master's degree in Environmental Studies from York University.

*Gordon Brent Ingram* was born on Vancouver Island and has degrees in environmental studies, photography, and ecosystem management. He completed his Ph.D. in environmental planning at the university of California, Berkeley, in 1989. He specializes in planning networks of protected areas and open space for the conservation of biological diversity on the remaining islands with tracts of primary rainforest in the Pacific Rim. He has been involved in research on and conservation of primary rainforest for 20 years. For the last 12 years he has conducted biodiversity surveys, environmental assessments, and open space analyses in over 20 countries and consults to a number of international organizations. He has taught at several universities and recently organized a human rights complaint against the University of British Columbia.

*Maurice Gibbons* was born in Peterborough, Ontario. He is a Professor Emeritus in Education at Simon Fraser University, holds a BA from the University of British Columbia, an MA in English Literature from the University of Washington and a Doctorate in Education from Harvard. A specialist in the development of innovative programs, he has written a number of articles and books about self-directed learning. He is currently a writer, publisher, exhibiting sculptor and consultant. On August 9, 1993, he was arrested at the Kennedy River Bridge and received a fine of $1250.00.

*Ronald B. Hatch* was born in Fort William, Ontario. He is presently Associate Professor in the Department of English, lecturing on Canadian literature and culture. He took his first degrees at the University of B.C.; his Ph.D. is from the University of Edinburgh. He has spent a number of years abroad as a Guest Professor, at Justus Liebig University and at the University of Erlangen-Nürnberg. He was arrested on August 9th at the Kennedy River Bridge.

*Loÿs Maingon*, a Killam fellow and interdisciplinary scholar, has worked extensively on the interpretation of nature in Western Civilization and environmental ethics. After completing a Ph.D. in 1983, he taught ecology as a cultural problem at the University of Western Ontario. Since 1992, he has taught in cross-cultural programmes concerning the status of nature and culture in First Nations and Caucasian cultures at U.B.C. He has lectured in the U.S. and Canada on deep ecology. He was arrested on August 9, 1993 at the Kennedy River Bridge.

*Christopher Hatch* was a civil disobedience trainer throughout the tumultuous summer of 1993. He was arrested on November 9th, arms locked into a cement barrel on the ramp leading onto the Kennedy River Bridge in Clayoquot Sound. He received his education in Scotland, France, Germany and Canada and holds an honours degree in Political Science from the University of British Columbia. He presently works for Greenpeace Canada on the campaign to end clearcutting worldwide.

*Marguerite Gibbons* was born in Maracaibo, Venezuela, and took her schooling in North Carolina. She has a degree in fine arts and received her teaching certificate from the University of Victoria. She has had three exhibitions of her paintings in the Vancouver area and has two more scheduled for 1995. She lives on Bowen Island with husband Maurice. On August 9, 1993, she was arrested at the Kennedy River Bridge and received a fine of $1250.00.

TO THE READER

If you are moved to write in support of the preservation of Clayoquot Sound, please contact:

The Premier of British Columbia
Legislative Buildings
Victoria, B.C.   V8V 1X4
Phone: 1-800-663-7867 or (604) 387-1715
Fax: (604) 387-0087

Minister of the Environment
Phone: (604) 387-1187
Fax: (604) 387-1356

Minister of Forests
Phone: (604) 387-6240
Fax: (604) 387-1040

If you wish further information on environmental issues in Clayoquot Sound, please contact:

Friends of Clayoquot Sound
P.O. Box 489
Tofino, B.C.   V0R 2Z0
Phone: (604) 725-4218
Fax: (604) 725-2527

Sierra Club of Western Canada
1525 Amelia Street
Victoria, B.C.   V8W 2K1
Phone: (604) 386-5255
Fax: (604) 386-4453

Greenpeace Canada
1726 Commercial Drive
Vancouver, B.C.   V5N 4A3
Phone: (604) 253-7701
Fax: (604) 253-0114

Nuu-chah-nulth Tribal Council
P.O. Box 1383
Port Alberni, B.C.   V9Y 7M2
Phone: (604) 724-5757
Fax: (604) 723-0463

Western Canada Wilderness Committee
20 Water Street
Vancouver, B.C.   V6B 1A4
Phone: (604) 683-8220
Fax: (604) 683-8229